ONE
NATION

MOSAICA PRESS

ONE
NATION

THE EMERGENCE & DEVELOPMENT
OF THE JEWISH PEOPLE

RABBI CHAIM BROWN

Mosaica Press, Inc.
© 2018 by Mosaica Press
Designed and typeset by Brocha Mirel Strizower

ISBN-10: 1-946351-33-4
ISBN-13: 978-1-946351-33-3

Published and distributed by:
Mosaica Press, Inc.
www.mosaicapress.com
info@mosaicapress.com

DEDICATED TO
GAD'L BEN YOSEF
DOVID HAKOHEN, Z"L

BY HIS DAUGHTER
ESTHER HARRIS

DEDICATED BY
CHESKY AND GITTY BROWN
AND FAMILY

TO MERIT SUCCESS IN ALL OF THEIR ENDEAVORS

DEDICATED IN HONOR OF OUR FATHER
HARAV DOVID YEHUDA
BEN BINYAMIN, Z"L

FROM THE BROWN FAMILY

הרב אהרן פעלדמאן
RABBI AHARON FELDMAN
421 YESHIVA LANE, APT 3A, BALTIMORE, MD 21208
TEL: 410-653-9433 FAX: 410-653-4694
STUDY: 410-484-7200 EXT. 114
EMAIL: RAF@COPPER.NET

ROSH HAYESHIVA
NER ISRAEL RABBINICAL COLLEGE

ראש הישיבה
ישיבת נר ישראל

בס״ד יט אדר תשע״ב
March 13, 2012

"One Nation" by Rabbi Chaim Brown traces the development of Emuna and Mitzvos as the purpose and the central theme of the world. He does this by citing how Chazal and their Meforshim view each of the major events and persons of the Torah, from Adam HaRishon until Matan Torah.

This *sefer* although small in its number of pages is large in its contribution to its readers by giving them a proper perspective on Torah and Mitzvos.

My *beracha* goes out to Rabbi Brown that his work be accepted by the Torah public and that he continue to benefit them with more such *seforim*.

With respects,

Aharon Feldman

Rabi Aharon Feldman

Table of Contents

ACKNOWLEDGMENTS

This *sefer* could not have been written without the contribution of many people who provided assistance along the way.

Poschin bi'chvod achsanya: Rav Yaacov Haber and Rabbi Doron Kornbluth and the rest of the Mosaica staff are deserving of utmost gratitude for the professionalism and expertise they demonstrated at every step along the way. Their eagerness to turn out a superior product never encroached on their true mission — to treat everyone with the utmost respect and honor. Hashem should bless them with continued success in their *avodas ha'kodesh*.

My father, Rav Dovid Brown, *zt"l*, instilled in his children and all who knew him a love for Hashem and His Torah. The greatness of his spirit continues to influence and guide all of us. And, *yibadel l'chaim*, my mother, Elaine Brown, the ultimate *lev tov*, continues to carry on my father's legacy. Her constant encouragement and support brings out the best in all of us. May she merit much happiness and *nachas* from the entire family and enjoy many years of health and happiness.

My in-laws, Rabbi Shmuel and Sury Bialik, embody the concept of self-sacrifice, always putting others before themselves. They should merit many years of health and happiness and *nachas* from their family.

My brothers Chesky and Eli and their families are a constant source of support. The publication of this *sefer* is no exception, and their support helped make its publication possible. May Hashem bless them with success in all of their endeavors and much blessing for the entire family.

My brother Rav Nochum generously made himself available throughout the process of producing the *sefer*. He constantly put his formidable writing skills and great Torah knowledge at my disposal. His constructive comments and critiques have enhanced this *sefer* considerably.

A number of eminent *talmidei chachamim* have reviewed and commented on portions of this *sefer*. In particular, Rav Baruch Kavin and Rav Aharon Deutsch took the time to review the entire manuscript, and their incisive comments helped make this a better *sefer*. Also, Mrs. Rephaella Levine greatly improved the *sefer* with her initial editing prior to its submission.

Acharonah acharonah chavivah to my wife, Shani, the embodiment of an *eishes chayil*, without whose encouragement and enthusiasm this work could not have been accomplished. She was always available as a listening ear and a sounding board for the ideas that form the basis of this *sefer*. May Hashem continue to grant us blessings and much *nachas* from our children.

INTRODUCTION

Hashem chose the Jewish People from all the nations in the world to be the *am segulah*, the treasured nation of Hashem. Why did Hashem choose only the Jewish People and no other nation? Why can't every nation be chosen, or at least every deserving individual among the nations be chosen?

Hashem chose Yisrael because their righteousness would endure forever. There have been many righteous non-Jewish people throughout the generations, but they were unable to pass this on to their descendants and their righteousness died with them. In contrast, the founder of the Jewish nation, Avraham, succeeded in passing his righteousness on to his descendants, as Hashem said, "For I know him that he instructs his children and his family after him so that they will guard the way of Hashem by engaging in charity and justice."[1]

Not only Avraham, but also Yitzchak and Yaakov built their own edifice of spiritual greatness, which they passed on to their descendants. The strength of the foundation ensures that the structure built upon it — i.e., the nation of Yisrael — will never topple.

Prior to Avraham, there were many righteous individuals, such as Sheis, Chanoch, Mesushelach, Noach, Shem, and Eiver. Yet, only the righteousness of Avraham endured for generations. What set Avraham apart from all of these great individuals? Avraham was unique in his faith in Hashem, which surpassed those that preceded him. Avraham's

---

1   *Parashas Vayeira* 18:19.

faith held fast through Ten Tests and never wavered. Avraham's faith in Hashem was sufficiently strong to become a hereditary trait that he would pass on to his descendants.

As descendants of our great forefathers, we bask in their merit. However, this merit sustained us only until the end of the First Holy Temple.[2] Thus, it was important for the Jewish People to earn their own merit as a nation as well. To accomplish this, Hashem exiled the Jewish People to Egypt and performed many miracles in the process of freeing them from subjugation and bringing them to Mount Sinai. This brought out the latent faith of the Jewish people. The Jewish nation reached the pinnacle of faith at Mount Sinai when they accepted the Torah, sight unseen, with the proclamation of "We will do and we will hear."[3]

The merit that we accrued as a nation at the foothills of Mount Sinai sustained us only as long as we remained a unified nation. When the unity of the Jewish nation was disrupted, as a result of the senseless hate that was prevalent at the end of the era of the Second Holy Temple, we were no longer a unified nation but a collection of individuals. This resulted in the destruction of the Holy Temple and the subsequent exile. However, even in our long exile, Hashem continues to sustain us in the merit of the greatness of our faith as individuals. In the darkest days of exile, our faith has not left us and we have never lost hope in our eventual redemption.

This greatness of faith is a testament to our origins; as descendants of our great ancestors, the drumbeat of faith in Hashem continuously pounds in our hearts. This is true not only for the righteous among us but even for the sinners. The Talmud tells us that even the sinners of Yisrael are filled with mitzvos like [the seeds] of a pomegranate.[4] Meaning, faith in Hashem is so inherent to the Jewish People that even the sinners are filled with faith in Hashem. And since faith is a constant mitzvah, the sinners are full of mitzvos.

---

2   *Maseches Shabbos* 55a.
3   *Parashas Mishpatim* 23:7.
4   *Maseches Sanhedrin* 37a.

However, in order to regain what we lost and merit the rebuilding of the Holy Temple, we need to rectify the sin of senseless hate and achieve the unity that was lost so many years ago. How do we regain this unity? We accomplish this by overcoming the divisions among us and bonding together in our service of Hashem. When we bond together as "one nation" and unite around a common cause and destiny, we set the stage for the arrival of Mashiach and the rebuilding of the Holy Temple.

In the following chapters, this *sefer* will explore the various stages of the development of the Jewish nation. This development was a gradual process, achieved in incremental steps, until its culmination with the giving of the Torah on Mount Sinai and the ultimate acceptance of the Oral Torah with the Purim story.

The prequel to these stages was the Garden of Eden. Adam and Chavah were a microcosm of the entire world, and had they not sinned, they would have received the Torah.

The first stage was the period following Adam and Chavah's expulsion from Gan Eden and prior to the *mabul*. In this stage, every person in the world had the opportunity to make himself deserving of being chosen by Hashem and earning the right to be called Yisrael.

The second stage is the post-*mabul* period. In this stage the world was divided into seventy nations, with one person — Avraham — chosen to be the forefather of the seventy-first nation: Yisrael.

In the third stage, Yitzchak and Yaakov were chosen to carry on Avraham's legacy at the expense of their brothers, Yishmael and Eisav.

In the next stage, the descendants of the forefathers would emerge from Egypt as a nation and would replicate the spiritual achievements of their forefathers.

In the final stage, the Chosen Nation would stand at the foot of Mount Sinai and receive the Torah from Hashem.

However, the acceptance of the Torah is not the final chapter. Our sages implore us to look at the Torah every single day as if we are receiving it that day. This means that we must constantly work on bolstering our faith so that every single day, we are reaffirming the age-old declaration of "We will do and we will hear." This is reflected in our fealty to the words of the sages and the rabbinic authorities of each generation, through whom the Sinaitic experience continues to be transmitted to the One Nation.

IN THE
BEGINNING

THEY SAW THAT THEY WERE BARE – EVEN THE
ONE MITZVAH THAT THEY HAD IN THEIR HANDS
HAD BEEN STRIPPED FROM THEM.
(BEREISHIS RABBAH 19:6)

INTRODUCTION TO STAGE I

The world was created for Yisrael and the Torah.[5] The Talmud tells us that Hashem created the world with a stipulation: "If Yisrael accepts the Torah, you will endure, but if not, I will turn you back into *tohu* and *vohu* (void and emptiness)."[6] Why did Hashem allow the entire existence of the world to dangle on an uncertain outcome? Hashem could have guaranteed the world's existence by forcing the Torah on Yisrael. Moreover, if the world was created for the Torah, why wasn't it given until 2,448 years after Creation?[7]

The Torah is a living entity, the vehicle of connection between Hashem and the Jewish People. The connection between Hashem and B'nei Yisrael is compared to a marriage.[8] A marriage is dependent on the commitment of the groom and the bride to each other. Similarly, the marriage of Hashem and Yisrael was contingent on the willingness of the nation of Yisrael to commit themselves to Hashem by accepting the marriage contract — i.e., the Torah and the mitzvos.

The connection between Yisrael and Hashem through the Torah can only be achieved through faith. A marriage is based on faith, as reflected in the blessing to newlyweds that they should merit building a *bayis ne'eman b'Yisrael* — a house of faith in Yisrael. Hashem refrained from giving the Torah to Yisrael until they had

---

5   *Rashi, Bereishis* 1:1.
6   *Maseches Shabbos* 88a.
7   *Rashi, Sanhedrin* 97a.
8   *Rashi, Parashas Yisro* 19:17.

the opportunity to attain the level of faith in Hashem necessary for an eternal bond.

Adam was a direct creation of Hashem, on the highest possible spiritual level, and as close to perfection as a human can be. This put him on the fast-track to receive the Torah. Yet, considering the above, Hashem did not give the Torah to Adam and Chavah immediately upon creation. Hashem first tested their faith with the one mitzvah they were given — the prohibition of eating from the *Eitz HaDaas* (Tree of Knowledge). Had Adam and Chavah passed this test and been faithful to this prohibition, they would have achieved the status of Yisrael and ultimately been given from the fruit of the *Eitz HaChaim* (the Tree of Life), which symbolizes the Torah — a tree of life for those who grasp onto it[9] and the source of eternal life.[10]

---

9   *Pirkei D'Rabbi Eliezer, perek* 12, based on *Mishlei* 3:18.
10   *Michtav Mi'Eliyahu.*

ONE MITZVAH: THE EITZ HADAAS

ashem created Adam and Chavah on the sixth day of Creation and He placed them in the Garden of Eden. He gave them only one mitzvah, the mitzvah of the *Eitz HaDaas*. Hashem commanded them, "From all of the trees in the garden you shall eat, but from the *Eitz HaDaas* of good and bad, you shall not eat from it, because on the day that you eat from it you will die."[11] Adam's task in the Garden of Eden was "to work it and guard it."[12] The Chafetz Chaim explains that Adam was not instructed to actually work on the trees of the Garden of Eden, which needed no work, but rather to "work" on the mitzvah that he was given.[13]

However, this mitzvah does not seem to require much work. Hashem planted many other fruit-bearing trees in the Garden of Eden that Adam and Chavah were permitted to eat, so it should not have been difficult for them to abstain from the fruit of the *Eitz HaDaas*. Nonetheless, successfully fulfilling this mitzvah would have brought Adam and Chavah eternal life. The commentators maintain that if Adam and Chavah had abstained from eating from the fruit of the *Eitz HaDaas* until Shabbos, they would have brought the world to completion and would have been

---

11   *Parashas Bereishis* 2:16–17.
12   Ibid. 2:15.
13   *Chafetz Chaim, Sefer Shem Olam, Shaar Hachzakas HaTorah*, chap. 10 in the footnotes.

given to eat from the *Eitz HaChaim* and merited eternal life.[14] What was the great achievement of abstaining from the *Eitz HaDaas* that would have brought Adam and Chavah eternal reward?

The mitzvah of the *Eitz HaDaas* challenged Adam and Chavah's faith. A closer look into the nature of the *Eitz HaDaas* sheds some light on the difficulty of this challenge. Rabbeinu Bachya maintains that the *Eitz HaDaas* was part of the same tree as the *Eitz HaChaim*, with the branches of one side of the tree comprising the *Eitz HaDaas*, and the branches of the other side, the *Eitz HaChaim*.[15] Also, the *Ohr HaChaim* says in the name of the *Zohar* that the Creator took a branch from the *Eitz HaDaas* and inserted it in the ground, and from that branch emerged all the other trees of the Garden of Eden.[16] Thus, all the trees in the Garden of Eden were connected, but only the *Eitz HaDaas* brought death. The other trees in the Garden were harmless and, in the case of the *Eitz HaChaim*, even brought eternal life.

This dichotomy was also found within the tree of the *Eitz HaDaas* itself. The Torah calls it "the Tree of Knowledge, good and bad."[17] The tree was bad — it brought death — but it had the potential to bring much good. If Adam and Chavah had abstained from eating from the *Eitz HaDaas* until Shabbos, the fruit of the *Eitz HaDaas* would have become permitted, and it would even have been used as an object of a mitzvah. Adam would have squeezed the fruit of the *Eitz HaDaas* and brought in the Shabbos by reciting Kiddush on its juice.[18]

It was difficult for Adam and Chavah to understand why the *Eitz HaDaas* was prohibited while the other trees in the Garden were permitted, despite being its offshoots. It was likewise inexplicable that the *Eitz HaDaas* was initially prohibited, considering it would eventually be used for a mitzvah. This ambiguity was Adam and Chavah's challenge in the mitzvah of the *Eitz HaDaas*. They were tasked with putting aside

---

14   Rabbeinu Moshe Chaim Luzzatto, *Sefer Daas Tevunos*.

15   *Parashas Bereishis* 2:9.

16   Ibid. 3:1.

17   Ibid. 2:9.

18   According to one opinion, the *Eitz HaDaas* was a grapevine, and even the dissenting opinions agree that it had some properties of a grapevine.

any misgivings they had about the mitzvah and to adhere to it without questioning it or otherwise interpreting it in any way.[19]

The challenge that Adam and Chavah faced could only be overcome with the attribute of humility. Acceptance of Hashem's commandments without understanding their purpose requires a heavy dose of humility. They would have to humbly accept the fact that despite their spiritual greatness as direct creations of Hashem, they did not have the capacity to understand Hashem's mitzvah, but were required nevertheless to fulfill it without any misgivings or hesitations.

Adam and Chavah naturally acted with exceptional character traits, as Shlomo HaMelech commented: "Hashem created Adam [to be] *yashar*."[20] What does it mean that Adam was created *yashar*? The *Ramban* explains that Adam naturally followed the path of *yashrus*,[21] and he exhibited exemplary behavior. What is the path of *yashrus*? The *Rambam* maintains[22] that the path of *yashrus* is the middle path; the path of moderation. One who always takes the middle path and eschews extreme behavior is considered to be a *yashar*. For Adam, *yashrus* was an inborn trait, and he naturally distanced himself from extreme behavior in all of his ways.

The path of *yashrus* is commendable for most character traits, but with respect to the trait of humility, Adam's inborn *yashrus* was not ideal. A *yashar* follows the middle path, but this is not the right path for the trait of humility. The Mishnah states: "One shall be exceedingly humble,"[23] and Rabbeinu Ovadiah of Bartenura[24] explains that although with regard to all other character traits one should follow the middle path, humility is an exception; one should distance himself to the extreme from the abominable character trait of haughtiness. The *Rambam* explains that this is because haughtiness, unlike most other attributes, is an affront not only to fellow man but also to the Almighty.[25] A haugh-

---

19   *Malbim, Parashas Bereishis* 2:16–17.
20   *Sefer Koheles* 7:29.
21   *Ramban, Parashas Bereishis* 2:9.
22   *Hilchos Deyos* 1:4.
23   *Pirkei Avos* 4:4.
24   Ibid.
25   *Hilchos Deyos* 2:3.

ty person is considered to have encroached on the Divine Presence, and therefore Hashem says about one who is haughty, "He and I can't live together in this world."[26] One who is haughty is so full of himself that he leaves no room for Hashem in his life.

Acting with humility was not only challenging because the middle path was not sufficient but also because of Adam's intrinsic greatness. According to the Vilna Gaon, Adam was especially challenged in the character train of haughtiness because he was a direct creation of Hashem. The Mishnah states: "Reflect upon three things and you will not come to sin: (1) Know from where you came, (2) to where you are going, and (3) before Whom you will in the future give a spiritual accounting. 'From where you came' — From a putrid drop."[27]

When one keeps in mind that he originates from a putrid drop, it keeps him humble.[28] Adam did not come from a putrid drop and thus was unable to use this as motivation to humble himself. This is what ultimately caused him to sin.[29]

Since Adam did not naturally distance himself sufficiently from any trace of haughtiness, Hashem commanded him in the mitzvah of the *Eitz HaDaas* to challenge him in this character trait. Rabbeinu Asher (the Rosh) maintains that Hashem prohibited Adam from eating from the *Eitz HaDaas* for the purpose of teaching him humility and reminding him of his Creator.[30] According to Rabbeinu Asher, there was no inherent difference between the *Eitz HaDaas* and the other trees in the Garden of Eden. Hashem prohibited Adam from eating the fruit of the *Eitz HaDaas* to remind him that he was not free to just do as he liked. He was obligated to adhere to the commandments of his Creator, whether he understood these commandments or not.

However, Rabbeinu Asher's contention that there was nothing inherently different about the *Eitz HaDaas* from the other trees in the

---

26   *Maseches Sotah* 5a.
27   *Pirkei Avos* 3:1.
28   Rabbeinu Ovadiah of Bartenura, ibid.
29   *Sefer Kol Eliyahu*, brought in *Sefer Matok Ha'Ohr* of Rav Eliyahu Levinstein.
30   *Peirush HaRosh, Parashas Bereishis* 3:11.

Garden of Eden appears to be contradicted by the midrash. The midrash states that Chavah gave from the fruit of the *Eitz HaDaas* to all the animals and birds of the world and they all ate from it except for a bird called the *chol*. All of the animals and birds became mortal except for the *chol*, which remained immortal.[31] The animals and birds were not commanded in the prohibition of the *Eitz HaDaas* and thus their mortality was not a punishment for defying Hashem's commandment but could only have been as a result of the toxic effects of the fruit of the tree.

The midrash that implies that the fruit of the *Eitz HaDaas* was toxic can be reconciled with Rabbeinu Asher's contention that the *Eitz HaDaas* was no different from the other trees in the Garden of Eden. Rav Shimshon Raphael Hirsch maintains that the prohibition of the fruit of the *Eitz HaDaas* fell into the same category as the prohibited foods of the Torah.[32] Thus, by gaining some insight into the prohibited foods of the Torah we can achieve some understanding of the prohibition of the *Eitz HaDaas* as well.

Some early commentators maintain that the Torah prohibits certain foods because these foods are detrimental to one's physical or spiritual well-being,[33] This seems to have support from the Talmud that states that nonkosher food items are *metamtem* (spiritually blemish) the heart.[34]

However, many commentators dispute this approach because the Torah is a spiritual guide, not a book of medicine or natural healing.[35] It may be true that the prohibited foods of the Torah are detrimental to our physical well-being, but that is not the reason for the prohibitions.[36] The *Maharal* posits that the Torah also does not prohibit foods because they are *metamtem* the heart, because there is nothing inherent about nonkosher food that causes spiritual harm; rather, it is the defiance of Hashem's commandment that causes harm. In the event that the

---

31   *Bereishis Rabbah* 19:5.

32   Commentary on the Chumash, *Parashas Bereishis* 3:16–17.

33   *Sefer HaChinuch*, mitzvah 73, *Ramban* and *Rabbeinu Bachya, Parashas Shemini* 11:13.

34   *Maseches Yuma* 39b.

35   *Abarbanel* and *Sefer Akeidas Yitzchak, Parashas Shemini* 11:13; *Kli Yakar, Parashas Shemini* 11:1.

36   *Maharal, Sefer Tiferes Yisrael*, chap. 8.

normally prohibited item becomes permitted, such as in a life-threatening situation, the item will cause no spiritual harm.[37]

The *Maharal* takes a similar approach with regard to the prohibition of *orlah* — the prohibition of eating the fruit of a newly planted tree for the first three years. According to the *Ramban*, the reason for the prohibition is that it is improper to partake of the fruit of a newly planted tree prior to bringing the first fruits to Yerushalayim as a thanksgiving to Hashem, as a fulfillment of the mitzvah of *neta revai* — the mitzvah to eat the fruits of a tree's fourth year in Yerushalayim. Since the fruits of the first three years are inferior, the Torah has us wait until the fourth year to bring the fruits to Yerushalayim, when the fruit is of sufficient quality to be offered to Hashem.[38]

The mitzvah seems quite straightforward and the chronology is easy to understand. However, the *Maharal* takes a contrary approach: He explains that it is not because of the inferiority of the fruit that the Torah prohibits us from eating the fruit of the first three years of the tree's life, but rather, the fruit is inferior because of the prohibition of *orlah*! Hashem does not want the tree to produce superior fruit while the fruit is prohibited because of the mitzvah of *orlah*![39] This teaches us that the mitzvos are not an outcome of the natural world, but rather the natural world conforms to the mitzvah. The midrash compares the mitzvah of the *Eitz HaDaas* to the mitzvah of *orlah*, which implies that the rationale behind the two mitzvos is the same.[40] Thus, although the *Eitz HaDaas* was no different from the other trees in the Garden of Eden, nevertheless, as a result of Hashem's prohibition of eating from its fruit, the *Eitz HaDaas* became toxic. The mitzvos create the reality in this world!

---

37   Ibid.
38   *Ramban, Parashas Kedoshim* 19:23.
39   *Sefer Nesivos Olam, Nesiv HaTzedakah, perek* 3.
40   *Vayikra Rabbah* 25.

ADAM AND CHAVAH were given only one mitzvah, the mitzvah of the *Eitz HaDaas*. Fulfilling this mitzvah would have brought them to spiritual completion. Their ability to perform this mitzvah was predicated on their humble acceptance of the mitzvah, on the basis of their faith in Hashem Who commanded it.

TWO

GUARDING THE MITZVOS: RABBINIC LAWS

dam was charged with transmitting the mitzvah of the *Eitz HaDaas* to Chavah, and while instructing her, he added an additional mitzvah, the prohibition of touching the tree.[41] The additional mitzvah served as a protective fence around Hashem's mitzvah, in the form of a Rabbinic mitzvah. The Torah vests the Torah sages of all generations with the authority to institute new statutes for the purpose of safeguarding the mitzvos from being breached. The Rabbinic edicts aid us in fulfilling the Torah mitzvos and prevent us from straying from the path of the Torah.

These mitzvos also help us connect with Hashem. The *Rambam*[42] states that the Torah instructs us: "To [Hashem] you shall cling." Chazal ask, "Is it possible for a person to cling to the Divine Presence when the Torah states, 'Hashem your G-d is [like] a consuming fire'?"[43] Chazal answer that the only manner in which to perform this mitzvah is by clinging to the sages and to their students.[44] The sages are the medium through which we connect with Hashem. By virtue of their righteousness and Torah scholarship, the sages are close to Hashem. When we learn Torah at the feet of the sages and adhere to their

---

41   *Parashas Bereishis* 3:3.
42   *Hilchos Deyos* 6:2.
43   *Parashas Va'eschanan* 4:22.
44   *Sifri, Devarim* 11:22.

directives, we attach ourselves to them, and by extension, we connect with Hashem.

Although the Rabbinic statutes were not given on Mount Sinai, they are from Hashem, no less than the mitzvos of the Torah. Hashem transmitted these mitzvos to the sages by means of *ruach hakodesh* — Divine inspiration. The Rabbinic mitzvos are the Divine will and should be fulfilled with the same reverence as the mitzvos of the Torah.[45] In some ways, the Rabbinic mitzvos are even more important than the Torah mitzvos as Shlomo HaMelech asserted,[46] "Your beloved [the decrees of the *rabbanim*] is better than wine [the 613 mitzvos of the Torah]."[47]

If the Rabbinic mitzvos are the Divine will, why didn't Hashem transmit the Rabbinic mitzvos on Mount Sinai together with the mitzvos of the Torah? Despite their importance, the Rabbinic mitzvos were not included in the transmission of the Torah on Mount Sinai because the Torah given directly by Hashem consists only of the eternal truth that can never be altered. The Rabbinic mitzvos, on the other hand, are limited to the generations that need them; some generations are more distant from Hashem or are more in need of safeguards than others. Generally, the earlier generations were on a high spiritual level and needed fewer safeguards. When the Torah was given on Mount Sinai, the Jewish People were on an exalted spiritual level and few Rabbinic mitzvos were needed. The Rabbinic mitzvos were added incrementally over the generations, as the sages — with Divine inspiration — deemed them to be necessary. The Rabbinic mitzvos increased over the generations because of the fundamental concept of *yeridas hadoros* — the steady decline of spiritual level as generations pass.

The reality of *yeridas hadoros* is true even for the greatest of Torah scholars. The great Torah sages were cognizant of the wide gulf between their own spiritual standing and that of the sages of previous generations. The Talmudic sage Rabbi Yochanan commented, "If the early sages were like angels, we are like people, and if the earlier generations

---

45   *Maharal, Sefer Be'er HaGolah Be'er 1, Sefer Tiferes Yisrael, perek 6.*

46   *Shir HaShirim 1:2.*

47   *Maseches Avodah Zarah 34a, Yerushalmi Sanhedrin 10:4.*

were like people, we are like donkeys."[48] The Talmud relates that Rabbi Yochanan was referring to the generation immediately preceding him![49] One consequence of the precipitous spiritual decline over the generations is that it became increasingly difficult to stay on the path of the Torah. The Rabbinic statutes instituted by the sages of every generation, to help keep the Jewish People on the right path, address this difficulty.[50]

The Rabbinic mitzvos remain in place only while still needed. Indeed, the Torah sages of one generation can overturn the Rabbinic mitzvos of a previous generation if they find that they are no longer necessary, provided that the latter sages are greater in number and wisdom than the sages who established them.[51] Thus, unlike the Torah, which is eternal, the Rabbinic mitzvos were only established for the generations that needed them.

Adam, as the direct handiwork of Hashem, was on a transcendent spiritual level and did not need Rabbinic mitzvos to achieve a connection with Him. However, Chavah was created from Adam and was not as closely connected to Hashem. Adam, as a prophet, transmitted to Chavah the Rabbinic edict to abstain from touching the tree. This edict protected Chavah from violating Hashem's mitzvah and helped her achieve a closer connection to Hashem through Adam.

---

48   *Maseches Shabbos* 112b.
49   Ibid.
50   *Maseches Shabbos.*
51   *Maseches Mo'ed Katan* 3b.

THE RABBINIC MITZVOS may not be stated explicitly in the Torah, but they are from Hashem just like the 613 mitzvos. Hashem designated some mitzvos as Torah mitzvos, and others as Rabbinic mitzvos, but all of the mitzvos are of Divine origin.[52]

---

52 *Maharal, Sefer Be'er HaGolah, Be'er* 1.

THREE

Adam and Chavah's Sin

Rav Shimshon Raphael Hirsch notes[53] that with the additional Rabbinic prohibition established by Adam, this one mitzvah of the *Eitz HaDaas* stood as the ultimate test of faith. It included all the elements that the evil inclination and the nations of the world find objectionable:

- It was a verbal tradition.
- It included a Rabbinic statute.
- It was a forbidden food.
- It was a *chok* — a prohibition without an obvious reason.

Rav Shimshon Raphael Hirsch says that the mitzvah of the *Eitz HaDaas* was especially challenging because it attracted both the physical and spiritual senses. All the human senses — the senses of taste, sight, imagination, and mind — were enticed by the attractive fruit that Hashem had prohibited.

The *Chasam Sofer*[54] maintains that the mitzvah of the *Eitz HaDaas* was more challenging for Chavah than it was for Adam. Adam heard the mitzvah directly from Hashem, which made it easier for him to fulfill the mitzvah despite not understanding it. Chavah heard the mitzvah from Adam, not directly from Hashem, and thus her inability to comprehend the mitzvah made it especially challenging. She was tasked with not only

---

53 Commentary on the Chumash, *Parashas Bereishis* 3:16–17.
54 *Teshuvos Chasam Sofer* §205.

maintaining her faith in Hashem who commanded the mitzvah, but also in remaining steadfast in her faith in Adam who transmitted the mitzvah.

The primordial Serpent stood in the way of Adam and Chavah faithfully fulfilling the commandment of Hashem. Who was this Serpent and why was it intent on seducing Adam and Chavah to sin? The *Zohar* equates the Serpent with Amalek.[55] Although the nation of Amalek did not yet exist, Amalek is not just a nation but a concept. The numerical value of Amalek is equivalent to that of *safek* (doubt), and anyone who plants doubt in our minds regarding Hashem's divinity or providence is called Amalek. Hashem placed the Serpent in the Garden of Eden to:

- challenge Adam and Chavah and force them to overcome obstacles in their quest to carry out Hashem's will;
- allow them to earn more reward, because *l'fum tzara agra* — the reward that one receives for the mitzvos is commensurate with the degree of difficulty in keeping them.

Hashem created man for the purpose of connecting to Him and developing a relationship of love with Him. As long as man is cognizant of Hashem's greatness and His providential care, he will instinctively love and fear his Creator, just as a child instinctively loves and fears his parents. However, Hashem allows man to act with free choice in order to make his efforts more meaningful and allow him to earn eternal reward. To that end, Hashem plants seeds of doubt about His greatness and providence in man's mind. At the time of Creation, Hashem assigned the primordial Serpent this task.

The Serpent concentrated its initial efforts on Chavah because she was not as closely connected to Hashem as Adam and thus more vulnerable to its seducements. It first targeted the Rabbinic mitzvah that safeguarded the prohibition of eating from the *Eitz HaDaas*. Tearing down the mitzvah's safeguard would make it possible for the Serpent to seduce Chavah into violating Hashem's prohibition. How did the Serpent accomplish this?

---

55 *Parashas Bereishis.*

The commentators explain that Chavah believed that the reason for Hashem's prohibition was that the *Eitz HaDaas* was toxic in some way and would prove lethal if its fruits were eaten.[56] Chavah did not perceive Adam's edict as a safeguard for Hashem's mitzvah but rather as an extension of the mitzvah. In her mind, Adam prohibited her from touching the tree because if the fruit was lethal, even touching the tree would cause harm.[57] The Serpent pushed her against the tree, causing her to touch it, and when she didn't feel any adverse effects, this cast doubt on the veracity of Adam's edict.[58]

Upon Chavah's breach of Adam's edict, Hashem's prohibition lost its safeguard and was left vulnerable and exposed. Furthermore, Chavah connected to Hashem through Adam and when she defied his edict her connection was weakened and she underwent a spiritual downfall. This emboldened the Serpent to sway Chavah about Hashem's mitzvah as well. It brazenly claimed that Hashem ate from the *Eitz HaDaas* in order to acquire the wisdom that allowed Him to create the world,[59] and that Hashem barred Adam and Chavah from eating from the fruit to prevent them from also acquiring this wisdom and, thereby, equal status with Him.[60]

The Serpent's brazen claim that Hashem considered man to be His adversaries and that the mitzvah of the *Eitz HaDaas* was for Hashem's good, not for man's good, was the opposite of the truth. Hashem created man for the purpose of achieving a relationship of love with Him and certainly not to be His adversaries. While Chavah was still closely attached to Hashem she would not have been vulnerable to this absurd contention, but her spiritual downfall allowed her to be seduced.

Chavah ate from the tree and then gave the fruit to Adam, and he too ate from the tree. How did the Serpent successfully convince Adam to

---

56   *Ramban, Parashas Bereishis* 3:6, also *Maharal, Gur Aryeh; Ohr HaChaim; Malbim; Chasam Sofer.*
57   *Maharal, Gur Aryeh, Parashas Bereishis* 3:4.
58   Although the Torah states that the Serpent pushed her against the tree, and thus she did not intentionally violate Adam's edict, many commentaries (*Maskil l'Dovid, Chasam Sofer, Sefer Toras Moshe*) maintain that she subsequently touched the tree willingly.
59   Ibid.
60   *Rashi, Parashas Bereishis* 3:6.

eat from the fruit of the *Eitz HaDaas*? After all, Adam heard the mitzvah directly from Hashem and knew that Hashem's mitzvah did not include a Divine prohibition to touch the tree, so he would not have been misled by the lack of consequences upon doing so. Moreover, Adam was closely connected to Hashem and certainly would not believe that Hashem considered him an adversary.

Adam was drawn to the *Eitz HaDaas* by the spirituality inherent in the tree. Hashem intended that the fruit of the tree would eventually be used for the mitzvah of Kiddush, and the sanctity of the tree emitted an enticing, fragrant scent.[61] Although the Serpent could not convince Adam to eat the fruit as an act of defiance against Hashem, it succeeded in convincing him that Hashem wanted him to eat the fruit despite the commandment to the contrary. How did it manage this?

Rav Meir Simcha of Dvinsk explains that the Serpent seduced Adam into believing that the prohibition of eating from the *Eitz HaDaas* was not to be taken at face value.[62] According to the Serpent, when Hashem prohibited Adam from eating from the *Eitz HaDaas* on threat of death, he was not actually banning Adam from the fruit, but just warning him of the consequences of eating from it. Thus, if Adam was willing to bear the consequences, he was permitted to eat from the tree. Adam rationalized that Hashem actually *wanted* him to eat from the *Eitz HaDaas*, but He wanted him to willingly give up his life for it. In other words, He wanted Adam to commit an act of self-sacrifice — but would not command Adam to do so. Adam concluded that not only was it *permissible* for him to eat the fruit, but it would actually be *commendable* to do so, and would bring him even closer to Hashem.

As mentioned, Adam's challenge was to fulfill the mitzvah with perfect faith, without questioning it, and certainly not to deduce his own interpretations. The spiritual allure of the fruit and Adam's overwhelming desire for spiritual growth blinded him to his true purpose in life, and made him vulnerable to the seducements of the Serpent. Instead

---

61   *Tzror HaMor, Parashas Bereishis* 3:6.
62   *Meshech Chochmah, Parashas Bereishis* 3:4–5.

of humbly fulfilling the commandment of his Creator, Adam justified defying His word in a distorted effort to bring himself close to Him.

Chavah's sin was a result of the mistaken belief that Hashem does not desire a connection with man. It is startling to note that Adam's sin was to seek out an even closer connection to Hashem. Their motivations seem to be polar opposites. But a closer look will reveal that Adam's sin was rooted in the same erroneous belief that man is inhibited in his quest to connect with Hashem from the earth. The Talmud tells us that Adam's height reached the heavens,[63] meaning that he was very close to Hashem,[64] but at the same time, his feet were firmly anchored on earth. Adam's sin was rooted in the belief that Hashem wanted him to give up his life for His mitzvah; that man's presence on earth inhibited him from forging an even greater connection with Hashem. Adam allowed himself to be persuaded that he could achieve a closer connection to Hashem by defying His mitzvah and giving up his life for Him. He did not believe he could achieve this while still living on earth.

This belief that man on earth is inhibited from connecting with Hashem was wrong. Everyone can connect. Actually, the reverse is true — man on earth can achieve a connection with Hashem that even the angels in heaven cannot achieve.[65] This can be accomplished by doing Hashem's will and adhering to His commandments, but certainly not by defying Him!

Had Adam and Chavah accepted the mitzvah of Hashem without any rationalizations and abstained from the fruit of the *Eitz HaDaas* until the onset of Shabbos,[66] they would have been strengthened in their faith and would have been given to eat from the *Eitz HaChaim*, thereby receiving the Torah and eternal life. However, they chose to rationalize the mitzvah and to eat from the tree despite the prohibition, and the result was death for themselves and all future generations. Adam not only lost the chance to bring the entire world to completion, but he fell

---

63   *Maseches Chagigah* 12a.

64   *Maharal, Gur Aryeh, Parashas Va'eschanan* 4:32.

65   Rabbeinu Bachya, *Parashas Eikev* 14:10.

66   The *Chasam Sofer* explains that the *Eitz HaDaas* was only forbidden until the onset of Shabbos (*Sefer Toras Moshe, Parashas Bereishis*). See also Rabbeinu Moshe Chaim Luzzatto. *Daas Tevunos, siman* 40; *Derech Hashem, siman* 3.

precipitously from his previous level. He descended into the abyss of coarse physicality and materialism, causing the Presence of Hashem — which had previously been very apparent in the world — to be hidden behind the facade of nature.[67] It was decreed in Heaven that Adam and his descendants would remain in this state until the consequences of the sin had run their course.[68]

---

67   *Meshech Chochmah, Parashas Vayechi* 50:10.
68   Rabbeinu Moshe Chaim Luzatto, *Daas Tevunos.*

FULFILLING THE MITZVAH of the *Eitz HaDaas* would have brought Adam and Chavah spiritual completion. However, the Serpent seduced them into thinking that the opposite was true — that defying the mitzvah would provide them with a spiritual boost. Their failure to fulfill this mitzvah shows us that even one who yearns for greater spirituality can still sin if he lacks proper perspective on the mitzvos.

AFTERWORD

Adam and Chavah's failure to trust wholeheartedly in Hashem rendered them unfit to receive the Torah,[69] because the acceptance of the Torah is predicated on faith in Hashem. Shlomo HaMelech commented: "Hashem created *adam* to be *yashar*, but he sought many calculations." What does it mean that Adam sought many calculations? Instead of simply accepting the mitzvah of Hashem on faith, Adam made calculations in an effort to comprehend the reason for the mitzvah. These calculations precipitated his downfall. Adam wanted nothing more than to serve Hashem in the most ideal way possible, but his calculations ultimately weakened his faith and caused him to transgress the mitzvah.

All of us, like Adam, are created with a natural tendency for *yashrus*, but following the path of *yashrus* can be a formidable challenge. Shlomo HaMelech commented: "There is a path of *yashrus* in front of man but it ends in the path of death."[70] The Vilna Gaon explains, "At times, a person takes a path that he believes to be *yashar*, but to his horror he finds that his chosen path actually leads him to his death." How does this happen? When a person makes too many calculations in his service, he weakens his faith in Hashem, and puts himself in danger of straying off the proper path. Conversely, when a person acts with perfect faith, he can be assured that he will follow the path of *yashrus* without being led astray.[71]

---

69   *Rashi, Sefer Yeshayah* 5:6, *Piyut* in Shavuos liturgy.
70   *Sefer Mishlei* 14:12.
71   Rabbeinu Eliyahu of Vilna, *Mishlei* 2:7, 11:3.

After the sin of Adam and Chavah, Hashem gave mankind the *Sheva Mitzvos B'nei Noach* — the Seven Noachide Laws. These logic-based mitzvos had the potential to put man back on the path of *yashrus* and enable him to receive the mitzvos of the Torah, which are called *yesharim* (just), as David HaMelech said, "The commandments of Hashem are *yesharim*, they gladden the heart."[72]

---

72   *Sefer Tehillim* 19:7.

B'NEI NOACH

AND HASHEM COMMANDED ADAM, SAYING:
"FROM ALL OF THE TREES OF THE GARDEN
YOU SHALL EAT." RABBI LEVI SAYS:
"HE WAS COMMANDED IN SIX MITZVOS...AVODAH
ZARAH, THE 'BLESSING' OF HASHEM, ESTABLISHING
A JUDICIAL SYSTEM, MURDER, FORBIDDEN
RELATIONS, AND THEFT."
(BEREISHIS RABBAH, PARASHAS BEREISHIS 17:6)

Introduction to Stage II

I n the aftermath of Adam's sin, Hashem withdrew from the world. Hashem's rule over the world remained unchanged, but His Presence (which had previously been very apparent in the world) was now obscured. At that time Hashem established the laws of nature.[73] This had the effect of masking the Hand of Hashem, and giving the impression that the events of the world occur on their own.[74]

Another consequence of the withdrawal of Hashem's Presence was the more material nature of Adam and Chavah's existence. Prior to his sin, Adam lived in the supernatural environment of the Garden of Eden, which provided for all his material needs and allowed him the luxury of occupying himself strictly in spiritual pursuits. The Garden of Eden required no upkeep; Adam ate from its trees and drank from its streams, and his garments were the Clouds of Glory.[75] However, after his sin, Adam was expelled from this ideal environment. Henceforth, Adam and his descendants would be forced to work for their daily bread.

Adam was born with a *bris milah*, but in the aftermath of Adam's sin, his *bris milah* was covered up.[76] The *bris milah* symbolizes the transcendence of nature. The Torah commands us to perform the *milah* on the eighth day of a boy's life because the number eight symbolizes the supernatural. Hashem created the natural world in seven days, and the

---

73   Ibid.
74   *Meshech Chochmah, Parashas Vayechi* 50:10.
75   Rabbeinu Bachya, *Parashas Bereishis* 2:9.
76   *Avos D'Rabbi Nosson* 2:5.

eighth day is beyond nature. The mitzvah of *bris milah* that is performed on the eighth day helps us transcend the natural world. By becoming an *arel* — one who lacks a *bris milah* — Adam was restricted to the confines of the natural world and distanced from Hashem.

The new environment that Adam and his descendants lived in would prove to be not only physically challenging but spiritually challenging as well. With Hashem's Presence obscured it became more difficult for people to recognize that the good they received was from Hashem. The eventual result was that the people turned away from Hashem and engaged in idolatry.

Nevertheless, even when Hashem's Presence is obscured, it is not completely hidden. If a person stops and observes, he can see the hand of Hashem orchestrating events behind the facade of nature. As the *Rambam* puts it, "When a person observes His great deeds and wondrous creatures and perceives His wisdom that cannot be measured and has no limit, he immediately praises and glorifies and harbors a great desire to know His great name."[77]

---

77   *Rambam, Hilchos Yesodei Torah* 2:2.

THE SEVEN NOACHIDE LAWS

A s we stated in the first section, the true reasons for the mitzvos of the Torah are hidden from human understanding, and the perceived reasons for the mitzvah should not be a factor in the performance of the mitzvah. Adam's sin of eating from the *Eitz HaDaas* demonstrated an inability to accept a mitzvah of Hashem unquestioningly, making him unfit to receive the mitzvos of the Torah.[78] Adam and his descendants would have to work to strengthen themselves in their faith in Hashem before they could be ready to receive the 613 mitzvos. In the meantime, they were commanded in the Noachide Laws. The Noachide Laws were given at this point as a transition stage until man could prove himself fit to accept the Torah's commandments.

The *Rambam*[79] states that Adam HaRishon was given six mitzvos: the prohibitions against

1. idolatry;
2. "blessing" Hashem (euphemism for cursing);
3. distorting justice;
4. murder;
5. forbidden relations;
6. theft.

---

78   *Rashi, Sefer Yeshayah* 5:6.
79   *Hilchos Melachim* 9:1.

From this, we can see that what is commonly referred to as the "Seven Noachide Laws" were originally only six mitzvos, and were initially given to Adam. Only the seventh mitzvah — the prohibition of eating the limb of a living animal — was first given to Noach.[80] This group of mitzvos, colloquially known as the *Sheva Mitzvos B'nei Noach*, are obligatory for all people at all times because they are rooted in fundamental civil behavior — *derech eretz*, which is a basic obligation for mankind.[81]

In this way, the mitzvos given to Adam are the opposite of the mitzvah of the *Eitz HaDaas*; the prohibition against eating from the fruit of the *Eitz HaDaas* transcended human logic and tested Adam and Chavah's faith, while the Noachide Laws are logical principles that society would have adopted even without Hashem's command.[82] The Noachide Laws govern life in the natural world, and thus the seven mitzvos correspond to the seven days of Creation of the natural world.

However, the prohibition against eating the meat of a still-living animal appears to be an outlier. Despite being one of the Seven Noachide Laws, it does not seem to be a logic-based mitzvah that society would have adopted on its own. Plenty of cultures have eaten and do eat parts of living animals. How does this mitzvah fit in with the other six?

The *Maharal* explains that the prohibition against eating the meat of a still-living animal is based on the concept of delaying gratification. This prohibition helps prevent the evil inclination from taking hold of a person and seducing him into transgressing the Noachide Laws. Eating the meat of a still-living animal is gluttonous behavior, for it shows that the person cannot stave off his own appetite even for the time it takes to end the animal's life. Such extreme indulgence provides entry to the

---

80   This is in accordance with the opinion of *Bereishis Rabbah* (*Parashas Bereishis* 17:6). However, according to the Talmud all seven mitzvos were given to Adam HaRishon (*Maseches Sanhedrin* 56b).

81   *Sefer Meshech Chochmah, Parashas Noach* 7:1.

82   *Sefer Chemdas Yisrael* on the *Rambam, Hilchos Melachim* 9:1.

evil inclination. Once a person habituates himself to instant gratification, it becomes difficult to summon the necessary self-discipline for the fulfillment of the other mitzvos. Thus, this mitzvah is foundational for the other six mitzvos.[83]

---

83 *Maharal, Sefer Gevuras Hashem*, chap. 66.

THE SEVEN NOACHIDE mitzvos are sensible and easy to understand. These mitzvos are less challenging to keep because of their comprehensibility and the social benefits that they provide. The Seven Noachide mitzvos were given to the world as a temporary measure until man would be fit to receive the Torah.

FIVE

THE GENERATION OF ENOSH

Chazal teach us that in the times of Enosh, the son of Sheis, the people began to engage in idolatry. As we said, after the sin of Adam, Hashem put the laws of nature into place, and these obscured His Presence. This made it more difficult for people to perceive the hand of Hashem orchestrating nature from behind the smokescreen, and eventually resulted in the people giving credit to false gods for the good they received.

The early idolaters did not engage in idolatry out of denial of Hashem's existence. They were cognizant of the dominion of Hashem in the world, but they erred in attributing independent power to the constellations. The *Rambam* explains: "The [generation of Enosh] believed that just as a mortal king wants his subjects to honor his servants, Hashem also wants His subjects to worship His servants (the stars), and that honoring them is tantamount to honoring Hashem. The [people] did not deny Hashem's existence but they were mistaken in their perception of the role of the constellations."[84]

The Chafetz Chaim explains[85] that the sin of the generation of Enosh was a consequence of their denial of Divine Providence. They believed that Hashem does not concern Himself with the occurrences of this world, and that He had ceded control of this world to intermediaries. This conviction was a consequence of the heretical belief that the

---

84   *Rambam, Hilchos Avodas Kochavim* 1:1.
85   *Sefer Shem Olam*, chap. 3.

occurrences in this world are too inconsequential for Hashem to involve Himself in. In fact, the reverse is true: because Hashem is the essence of good, He concerns Himself most with those who are in need. The Talmud declares, "Anywhere you find the greatness of Hashem, that is where you find His humility."[86] Hashem's Presence is with the ill and with anyone who is humbled and downtrodden.[87] Thus the greatness of Hashem does not mean that He cedes control over the minutiae of the world; rather, His greatness lies in His humility, in that He is most concerned with the beings in this lower world.

In subsequent generations the people took the belief of Enosh's generation one step further and began to craft wooden and stone images of the stars, which became the objects of their worship. This further distanced them from Hashem, and with the passage of time, the people began to believe in the divinity of the constellations. This belief became so pervasive that eventually only select individuals in each generation served Hashem, such as Chanoch, Mesushelach, Noach, Shem, and Ever.[88]

---

86   *Maseches Megillah* 31a.
87   *Maharal, Sefer Nesivos Olam, Nesiv Ha'Anavah, perakim* 1–2.
88   *Rambam, Hilchos Avodas Kochavim* 1:2.

THE LAWS OF nature make it challenging to recognize Divine Providence. Most people denied Divine Providence and credited false gods for the good they received. Only those who made the effort to look beyond the mask perceived the hand of Hashem orchestrating nature.

SIX

THE MABUL

A
s we have seen, the concealment of the Divine Presence
and the misconceptions that were introduced in the generation of Enosh ultimately led to idolatry. With Divine
Providence concealed behind the facade of nature, it became a difficult challenge to recognize the goodness of Hashem. Only
a few rare individuals, such as Mesushelach and Chanoch, managed to
perceive the hand of Hashem orchestrating nature, while the masses
remained in darkness. Hashem did not intend the world to remain in
this state indefinitely, as He is all-merciful and wanted to give everyone the opportunity to recognize and worship Him.

In the tenth generation after Adam's sin — the generation of Noach —
Hashem pulled back the curtain and removed the facade of the laws of na-
ture. Hashem's Presence now became felt more strongly in the world, and
His direct influence resulted in a more robust and prolific environment.
In this generation, the earth began to produce in a way that had not been
seen since before Adam's sin. The curse that Adam received after his sin —
"With the sweat of your brow you shall eat bread"[89] — began to reverse,
along with the curse that the earth would "sprout thorns and thistles."[90]
The people lived in a veritable Garden of Eden and they were no longer
forced to work hard for their daily bread.[91]

---

89   *Parashas Bereishis* 3:19.
90   Ibid. 3:18.
91   My father, *z"tzl*, in *Mysteries of Creation*, p. 114, Targum Press.

The midrash gives us insight into the remarkably blessed conditions enjoyed by the generation of Noach: "The generation of the Great Flood planted only once every forty years, and the crops grew continuously. Their children never died young, they were huge and were capable of walking from one end of the world to the other in a brief time. They uprooted trees with their bare hands; lions and leopards were no more a nuisance than thorns, and the climate was one of perpetual springtime."[92]

The curses Chavah received also began to reverse. The midrash relates: "The women gave birth twice a year and each time they gave birth to quadruplets or quintuplets. A child was capable of walking outdoors on the day of his birth. Women delivered children after one day of pregnancy, or according to another opinion, after three days of pregnancy. When a child was born, he was immediately capable and his mother would request from the newborn, 'Bring me a flint to cut your cord.'"[93] This most favorable environment was a return to the Garden of Eden-like lifestyle that Adam and Chavah lived in prior to their sin.

The enviable conditions that the people enjoyed should have made them cognizant of Hashem and His goodness, but their abundant lifestyle made them haughty, which turned them against Hashem. The people continued to engage in idolatry, but, in contrast to the people of previous generations who did so because Hashem's Presence was hidden, the people of this generation willfully blinded themselves to His Presence. Wealth can blind a person from Hashem's Presence even when it is apparent,[94] especially when the wealth is received without much effort.[95] Excessive wealth has two potential detrimental effects:[96]

- It can draw a person into excessive physical desires, which can make him forget Hashem. The Torah warns us: "Lest you eat and be satiated and build good houses...and everything you

---

92   *Bereishis Rabbah* 34:11.
93   *Aggadas Bereishis* 310.
94   *Alshich* 1:1, Rabbeinu Bachya, *Parashas Eikev* 8:14.
95   *Seforno, Parashas Va'eschanan* 6:10–12.
96   *Hagahah*, ibid., Cooperman edition.

have increases. And your heart becomes haughty and you forget Hashem your G-d."[97]

- It can make a person haughty and instill in him the belief that it
  was his own abilities and talents that made him wealthy, as the
  Torah warns: "And you will say in your heart, 'My strength and
  the power of my hand produced for me this wealth.'"[98]

No one is immune to the pernicious effects of wealth. This can be
seen from the sin of the Golden Calf, which occurred soon after the
Torah was given at Mount Sinai. The Talmud tells us that Moshe
blamed this sin on the wealth that the Jewish People accumulated after
the drowning of the Egyptians in the Yam Suf.[99] No group of people
had experienced the Presence of Hashem with the same clarity as the
Jewish People at the Yam Suf. The midrash tells us that a maidservant
at the Yam Suf saw [a vision of Hashem] that even Yechezkel ben Buzi
[the prophet who saw the Holy Chariot of Hashem] did not see.[100] Yet
the wealth that they accumulated in the immediate aftermath of the
splitting of the Yam Suf ultimately caused them to craft a golden calf as
an object of their worship.

Thus, we see that wealth has the effect of making a person forget
Hashem even when His Presence is apparent in the world. This is
because abundant materialism makes a person haughty, which turns
him away from Hashem. An arrogant person is so full of himself that
he leaves no room for Hashem. We find that Hashem says about the
haughty, "I and he cannot live together in the world."[101] Hashem doesn't
live together with the arrogant person because his arrogance doesn't
allow him to make space for Hashem.

This is what occurred in the generation of Noach. The abundant materialism that the generation of Noach enjoyed made them haughty and
blinded them to Hashem's Presence. The people became so arrogant and

---

97   *Parashas Eikev* 8:12–14.
98   Ibid. 8:17.
99   *Maseches Berachos* 32a.
100 *Mechilta, Parashas Beshalach.*
101 *Maseches Sotah* 4b.

boastful that they claimed they had no need for Hashem's goodness, not even the rain, because they could bring down the rain themselves by sewing the clouds.[102]

Thus, despite the bounty that the people enjoyed, and the gratitude they should have had for all the good that Hashem bestowed upon them, they rebelled against Him. They defied Hashem and the mitzvos He gave them, as the Torah states: "And Hashem saw that the people on Earth were very wicked."[103] The people were steeped in the sins of idolatry, immoral relations, and above all, the sin of theft.[104]

With this failure, there was no longer any hope that the people would recognize Hashem and the good that He does. The people had failed to recognize Hashem in both good times and bad. When Hashem had hidden His face in the aftermath of Adam's sin, they turned away from Him and worshipped the intermediaries. When Hashem's Presence was more strongly felt in the world, the people enjoyed the fruits of Hashem's goodness but failed to recognize Him because the abundance they enjoyed blinded them to His Presence.

Hashem decreed that the people of the world would be destroyed in a deluge. Since Hashem is all-merciful, He did not carry out this decree right away so that the people would have a chance to repent. Hashem gave the people ample warning of the impending catastrophe, but the threat of annihilation did not serve the purpose of humbling the people and bringing them to repentance. They dismissed the threat of extermination with the boast that they could prevent the subterranean water from rising and flooding the earth by plugging the openings of the earth with their feet.[105]

Hashem punished the generation of Noach measure for measure; He annihilated the people with the very goodness for which they were so ungrateful. He brought down the rain relentlessly until the entire earth was submerged in water. But even after the rain commenced, Hashem's

102 *Pirkei D'Rabbi Eliezer, perek* 22.
103 *Parashas Bereishis* 6:5.
104 *Rashi, Parashas Noach* 6:11.
105 *Pirkei D'Rabbi Eliezer, perek* 22.

mercy remained. The rain initially came down in a merciful manner, which gave the people the opportunity to repent, but when this did not occur the rain turned into a deluge.[106]

Of course, the world was not completely destroyed; it would be rebuilt through Noach and his sons. Noach was a righteous person who distanced himself from the arrogant ways of his generation.[107] In contrast to his fellow men, Noach walked with Hashem.[108] Why did Noach, out of all people in the world, recognize Hashem? Noach's humility distinguished him from all others and allowed him to see Hashem. The Torah states that Noach was *tamim* — which means he was humble.[109] Noach's humble ways allowed him to recognize Hashem and saved him and his family from the destruction of the *mabul*.

---

106   *Rashi, Parashas Noach* 7:12.
107   *Ramban, Parashas Noach*, 6:9.
108   *Parashas Noach* 6:9.
109   *Rashi, Maseches Avodah Zarah* 6a.

WEALTH CAN POTENTIALLY make a person haughty and blind him to Hashem's Presence. This is what occurred to the generation of Noach, whose great wealth made the people arrogant. The antidote to the challenge of wealth is humbleness. Only a humble person, such as Noach, can recognize that his wealth is a blessing from Hashem and not a result of his own abilities.

SEVEN

THE POST-MABUL WORLD

The devastation left in the wake of the deluge was profound; even the stones of the mills dissolved and one cubit of the earth's surface was wiped away.[110] Considering that Noach and his children were to continue living in the world after the deluge, why did Hashem find it necessary to destroy its contents? He could have killed the inhabitants while leaving the contents of the world intact!

The explanation is enlightening. Hashem did not want the people of the world to ever face the same test as the generation of Noach, who enjoyed great bounty but became arrogant and distant from Hashem as a result. Hashem determined that it was not in man's interest to have too much good, as Shlomo HaMelech pleaded, "Poverty and wealth do not give me. Provide me with my regular bread; lest I be satiated and I deny and I say, 'Who is Hashem?'"[111] Hashem could have accomplished this by obscuring His Presence from the world as He did in the aftermath of Adam's sin, but this could have led to idolatry as it is did in the generation of Enosh. Instead, Hashem wore away the earth with the boiling waters of the deluge that were mixed with sulfur, which permanently weakened the earth and ensured that it would never again produce in the same way it did previously.[112] This guaranteed that the people of the world would never again become as haughty as the generation of Noach.

---

110 *Bereishis Rabbah* 28:3.
111 *Sefer Mishlei* 30:8–9.
112 My father, z"tzl, in *Mysteries of Creation*, p. 114, Targum Press.

Hashem effected another notable change in the aftermath of the deluge. The sun's relative position to the earth changed:[113] Prior to the deluge, the sun moved parallel to the equator, which led to the perpetual springtime that the inhabitants of the earth enjoyed. The strong sunlight had been the source of the fruitfulness of the land and the longevity of its inhabitants. After the deluge, Hashem realigned the position of the sun so that its movement deviated from the equator.[114] This resulted in a weakened land and a decreased harvest compared to the previous state of affairs.

After the deluge, Hashem promised Noach that He would never again devastate the world in the same way, not just by water but also not by fire or any other means.[115] Why did Hashem make this promise? Hashem grants everyone free will to follow the path of his choice, so how could it have been a certainty that it would never again be necessary to destroy the world? The answer is that with the new weakened state of the world, man would never again be blessed with the optimal conditions that existed previously. Without such abundance, the people would never reach the heights of arrogance of the generation of Noach, which was the primary cause of their rebellion against Hashem.

However, the lack of abundance can also be a challenge, as Rabbi Moshe Chaim Luzzatto says: "All circumstances in this world test a person; poverty on the one hand and wealth on the other."[116] While nothing blinds a person to Hashem's Presence as much as wealth, nevertheless, even in the absence of great abundance, it is still possible for man to rebel against Hashem. Certainly, even after the Great Flood there were people who continued to rebel against Hashem, but

---

113 *Seforno, Parashas Noach* 8:22.

114 The *Seforno's* words imply that since the *mabul*, the sun moves around the earth on a "*galgal noteh m'kav mashve hayom*," lit., a circle deviating from the equator line. According to contemporary understanding, we would refer to the tilt of the earth on its axis so that it is not parallel to the sun, which is the source of the seasons in the Northern and Southern latitudes. The perspective may differ, but the result is the same; the light of the sun is not uniformly intense as it shines on the Earth.

115 *Maseches Zevachim* 116a.

116 *Sefer Mesilas Yesharim, perek* 1.

importantly, a rebellion on the scale of the generation of Noach would never recur.

To ensure that a mass rebellion of even a small scale would never again occur, Hashem determined that He would divide mankind into seventy nations. Hashem established seventy angels in heaven who were given the future task of administering the seventy nations-to-be.[117] Each nation would be placed under a *mazal* (zodiac), which would shape the nation's identity and temperament. Each *mazal* influences the nations under its sphere of influence in a unique way.[118] Consequently, the peoples of the world would have very divergent natures, which would make mass rebellion implausible.

However, this would not occur immediately after the deluge. It would take many years to build a critical mass of people that were sufficient to be divided up into seventy nations. Moreover, Hashem wanted to establish a seventy-first nation that would not be placed under a specific *mazal* but would be directly under Hashem. Thus, mankind could not be divided into seventy nations until a righteous person emerged, who would prove himself to be fit to be the forefather of the seventy-first nation.

The weaker sun and less fertile earth made it less likely for people to become haughty and rebel against Hashem to the degree that occurred prior to the *mabul*. The differing natures of the nations ensured that even when one nation rebelled against Hashem, other nations would not. With the certainty that there would never again be a mass rebellion Hashem promised that He would never again annihilate the entire world. Still, He did not vow not to devastate any individual nation, because it was certainly possible that one nation would rebel against Hashem.[119] For instance, Hashem

- overturned Sodom;
- instructed the Jewish People to destroy the seven nations of Canaan;
- drowned the Egyptians in the Yam Suf.

---

117   *Netziv, Sefer Ha'amek Davar, Parashas Haazinu 32:8.*
118   *Maharal, Sefer Ohr Chadash.*
119   *Rashi, Parashas Shemos 1:10.*

These nations were destroyed because their sinful nature made their continued existence untenable. But they were individual nations; Hashem did not need to destroy the entire world.

It is fitting that Hashem made the rainbow as a symbol of His vow to never again destroy the world with a *mabul*. The Talmud tells us that when Hashem seeks to destroy the world, the rainbow appears as a reminder of this vow. There are seven colors of the rainbow, known as the visible spectrum: red, orange, yellow, green, blue, indigo, and violet. The multicolored rainbow is a reminder that the world consists of a vast array of diverse people who come in all stripes and colors. Since the people of the world are so different, even when some rebel against Hashem, others are fulfilling His will, and so the world prevails. [120]

Rav Shimshon Raphael Hirsch elaborates: Hashem promised to never again destroy the world as a result of the deeds of the wicked because the presence of the righteous serves to balance out the deeds of the wicked. The rainbow is one complete ray of white light refracted into seven degrees of seven colors, from the red rays to violet. The seven rays of light signify that all of humankind, from the most righteous to the wicked, from the red to the violet, together form one complete pure white ray. Hashem binds all mankind together because all are fragments of one light, refracted rays of the one spirit of G-d, and even the lowest, most distant one is still a son of light.

---

120   This also helps assure the Jewish People's survival; they have survived in their long exile against all odds, since when one nation expels them there will always another nation to take them in.

HASHEM PROMISED TO never again annihilate the entire world. The great kaleidoscope of people on planet Earth guarantees their survival. The breathtaking diversity of the people ensures that when one nation rebels against Hashem, other nations will not follow suit.

EIGHT

THE CONCEPT OF YISRAEL

Placing the nations under the *mazalos* gave each nation a unique identity, but it also had the adverse effect of distancing the people from Hashem. The *mazalos* act as a buffer between Hashem and the nations of the world and preclude a direct relationship with Him. The institution of the *mazalos* guaranteed the survival of the world, but also did not allow for the true purpose of Creation, for man to develop a relationship of love with Hashem.

Therefore, Hashem established the concept of a seventy-first nation, to be designated as Yisrael, which would not be placed under any *mazal*. The nation of Yisrael would bask directly under the Divine Providence,[121] without anything to interfere with its relationship with Hashem. This allowed Yisrael the possibility of cleaving to Hashem, which was not possible for any other nations.

The nation that would be designated Yisrael would receive the holy land of Eretz Yisrael, the only place where they could develop to their full potential. Eretz Yisrael was the one place where the earth retained its original pre-deluge strength. The midrash relates that the waters of the deluge rained down on the entire world except for of Eretz Yisrael.[122] The underground water did not rise up underneath Eretz Yisrael and

---

121 *Ramban, Parashas Acharei Mos* 18:25; Rabbeinu Bachya, *Eikev* 11:12; *Gur Aryeh, Parashas Lech Lecha* 17:8.
122 *Pirkei D'Rabbi Eliezer, perek* 23.

the torrential rains of the Great Flood did not batter it.[123] The trees were not uprooted and the land's surface was not washed away. Although the waters of the deluge entered Eretz Yisrael from other lands,[124] because the water did not fall directly on Eretz Yisrael it did not have the same devastating effect that it had on other lands. The *Ramban* explains that the olive leaf grasped by the the dove that Noach sent from the ark was taken from the olive trees of Eretz Yisrael that survived the deluge.[125] The existence of the olive leaf demonstrated that Eretz Yisrael was no longer submerged in water and that the world was beginning to recover from the deluge.

Furthermore, the new positioning of the sun, which had such a deleterious effect on most of the world, did not have the same effect on Eretz Yisrael. Even after the deluge, Eretz Yisrael maintained its temperate climate without the extreme climate changes of most other lands. Rabbeinu Bachya maintains that the world is divided into seven regions, with seven different climates. Eretz Yisrael is in the middle region, which has a temperate climate that is appealing to all people.[126] David HaMelech sang about the beautiful climate of Eretz Yisrael, "It is a beautiful climate, the joy of all lands."[127]

Since the Great Flood and its aftermath did not impact Eretz Yisrael as much as other lands, it retained much of its original pre-flood fertility. This is positive, of course, but Hashem weakened the earth for a reason: to ensure that the earth's bounty would not cause the people to become haughty and rebel against Him. Thus, the benefits of living in Eretz Yisrael were potentially spiritually detrimental because it put the residents of Eretz Yisrael at risk of becoming haughty and turning against Hashem. This is exactly what occurred to the seven nations of Canaan whose degenerate behavior was worse than that of all other nations.[128] This is also what occurred to the cities of Sodom and Amorah,

---

123   *Ramban, Parashas Noach* 8:11.
124   Ibid.
125   Ibid.
126   *Parashas Eikev* 8:7.
127   *Sefer Tehillim* 48:3.
128   *Toras Kohanim, Parashas Acharei Mos* 18:3.

whose inhabitants became haughty and wicked as a result of living on the especially lush and fertile region of Eretz Yisrael.[129]

As a result of their wickedness, Hashem decreed that the residents of Sodom and Amorah along with three other cities in their district were to be destroyed without a trace. As was the case in the deluge, Hashem deemed it insufficient to kill the inhabitants of Sodom and Amorah without destroying the cities themselves. Since the fertility of the region contributed to their sins it was imperative to destroy the land, lest it cause future generations to sin in the same way. Hashem brought upon Sodom and Amorah sulfur and fire and overturned the cities. The sulfur that Hashem used in the destruction of the cities was the same agent that Hashem mixed in the waters of the Great Flood. The caustic sulfur stripped the land of its fertility and thus removed the danger for its future inhabitants.

The other regions of Eretz Yisrael remained intact because although it was a blessed land flowing with milk and honey, it was not as lush as Sodom and Amorah and did not pose the same spiritual danger. Still, in order to thrive in Eretz Yisrael and avoid the spiritual trap that its bounty posed, its rightful inhabitants (Yisrael-designate) needed to be specially adapted to this special land. The nation of Yisrael are characterized by two important traits that would make them immune from the adverse effects of the land's abundance. The two traits are:

- Humility, which would prevent their wealth from blinding them to Hashem's Presence.
- Gratitude, which would prevent them from rebelling against Hashem, the source of all the goodness that surrounded them.

Among all the nations of the world, only the Jewish nation possessed a sufficient measure of humility and gratitude to overcome the challenge of the material abundance of Eretz Yisrael, as the Torah states, "It is not because you are the most numerous of all the nations that Hashem desired and chose you, because you are the fewest of all the

---

129   *Parashas Lech Lecha* 13:10.

nations."[130] *Rashi* explains this verse to mean that Hashem chose Yisrael because they don't become haughty when blessed with an abundance from Hashem.[131]

To prevent any other nation from facing the challenge of Eretz Yisrael, Hashem obliterated the earth of Eretz Yisrael with salt and sulfur after the exile of the Jewish nation upon the destruction of the Second Holy Temple.[132] This was a fulfillment of the verse, "Sulfur and salt, an inferno of the entire land, it will not be planted and it will not sprout and no grass will grow from it, like the upending of Sodom and Amorah, Admah and Tzvoyim, that Hashem overturned with his anger and wrath."[133] Hashem devastated Eretz Yisrael with the caustic agent of sulfur in the same way He had destroyed Sodom and Amorah so many years before. This ensured that any other nations that would take up residence in Eretz Yisrael after the Jewish nation was exiled would not face the challenge of a fertile land flowing with milk and honey.

---

130   *Parashas Va'eschanan* 7:7.
131   *Rashi*, ibid.
132   *Maseches Yuma* 54a.
133   *Parashas Nitzavim* 29:22.

HASHEM SPARED ONE land from the devastation of the Great Flood — Eretz Yisrael. This land would be reserved for the one nation that would not be adversely affected by the abundance available in the land that flowed with milk and honey. Only the nation of Yisrael, who is blessed with the twin traits of humility and gratitude would be up to the task.

NINE

SEPARATION OF THE NATIONS

THE GENERATION OF THE HAFLAGAH: SEVENTY VS. ONE

As we said, Hashem determined after the Great Flood that mankind would be divided into seventy nations and would be placed under the influence of the *mazalos*. One nation — the seventy-first nation — would not be placed under the *mazalos* and instead would be under the direct influence of Hashem. This nation would be designated the Chosen Nation and would receive the Torah at Mount Sinai. However, the designation of the Chosen Nation and the division of mankind into seventy nations did not occur for many years after the deluge, because the people were not yet numerous enough to be divided into nations. Moreover, since placing the nations under the *mazalos* distanced them from Hashem, this could only occur when they proved themselves unworthy of a close relationship with Hashem. Also, the division of the nations could occur only with the appearance of a righteous person with the necessary characteristics to be the forefather of the Chosen Nation.

The person who proved himself worthy of becoming the forefather of the Chosen Nation was Avraham Avinu. At the same time that Avraham was distinguishing himself as deserving of the mantle of the forefather of Yisrael (see next chapter), the rest of humanity was acting in a manner that made it patently clear that they were unfit for this role. When

Avraham was fifty-two years old, the people of his generation sinned by attempting to build a tower that reached to the heavens. This was a great sin that resulted in the actualization of the preordained decree, and mankind was divided into seventy nations.

Why was the building of the tower regarded as such an egregious sin? The midrash elaborates:

> *The people spoke brazen words against Hashem and Avraham. They mocked Avraham; they called him a childless mule who would never give birth. They spoke against Hashem and said, "It is not right that [Hashem] chose for Himself the heavens and gave us the [earth] down here. Let us make a tower and put an idol on top, and place a sword in its hand, and it will appear as if we are waging battle with Him."* [134]

The *Sefer Yefei To'ar* explains that the people were in denial of Divine Providence. They believed that Hashem had abdicated His rule over the world and given it over completely to the *mazalos*. Convinced that Hashem had abandoned them to their fate, they rebelled against Him and threw off the yoke of the mitzvos. The scheme to place an idol on a tower with a sword in its hands indicated that they deemed themselves to be at war with Hashem, symbolizing their defiance of His authority.

The people's belief that the world had been given over to intermediaries sheds further light on the sin of that generation — the generation of the *Haflagah*. (*Haflagah* means a split, i.e., in this generation the people were split up into distinct nations.) *Rashi* comments: "The people said that once every 1,656 years the heaven collapses, just as it occurred at the time of the deluge — let us make supports for it." [135] The *Maharal* explains that the people thought that the deluge had occurred as a result of the movement of the constellations, and since it occurred 1,656 years after Creation, it would reoccur after the same lapse of time. [136]

---

134 *Bereishis Rabbah* 38:6.
135 *Rashi, Parashas Noach* 11:1.
136 *Gur Aryeh*, ibid.

The people were partially correct, as the Talmud tells us that the deluge occurred as a result of the movement of the constellations.[137] However, there was a vast difference between their view and the reality of what occurred. The movement of the constellations that brought the deluge was not some random event that occurred without Hashem's direct involvement. Hashem moved around the constellations as a mechanism for bringing the deluge as a punishment for man's wicked deeds. In contrast, the view of that generation was that the deluge occurred by chance unrelated to their deeds, which was a denial of the Divine Providence and the concept of reward and punishment. This conviction was an outgrowth of their belief that Hashem did not concern Himself with the occurrences of this world, and that He had given over the world to intermediaries.[138]

The belief of this generation, that Hashem had given over the world to intermediaries, made their punishment especially apt; they were divided into seventy nations, with each nation placed under the authority of their specific *mazal*. As such, their denial of Divine Providence was a self-fulfilling prophecy; they were, in fact, placed under the authority of the *mazalos* and were no longer under the direct influence of Hashem.

It is important to note that even after the people were placed under the *mazalos*, Divine Providence was still in place and Hashem had not abdicated His rule over the world. Nevertheless, a new reality took hold with regard to Divine Providence. Previously, every individual merited Divine Providence, but after Hashem divided up the people into nations and placed each nation under its *mazal*, this was no longer the case. Only nations as a whole would merit Divine Providence but not individuals among the nations.[139] Individuals among the nations were subject to random occurrences as portended by the *mazalos*.

The one exception to this rule was the seventy-first nation. The nation of Yisrael would not be administered by the *mazalos* or an angel, but rather would be placed directly under Divine Providence. Consequently,

---

137   *Maseches Rosh Hashanah* 11b.

138   *Sefer Me'am Loez*, ibid.

139   *Sefer Mei HaShiloach, Parashas Bamidbar*.

a Jewish person merits individual Divine Providence in accordance with his deeds and is not subject to random events at all.[140] Consistent with this, the Mishnah tells us that every Jewish person shall say, "The world was created for me."[141] This is because Divine Providence is focused on every Jewish individual as if he is an entire world. However, Yisrael's privileged status as the only nation under the direct rule of Hashem is a double-edged sword. All other nations have the support of their individual *mazal* that shapes their identity and acts as a pipeline to funnel them their material needs irrespective of their merits.[142] In contrast, Yisrael is not overseen by any *mazal* and receives material goods directly from Hashem. This is dependent on their merits, however, and when they do not follow the path of the Torah, Hashem cuts them off and they find themselves more bereft than any other nation.

The lack of a *mazal* also means Yisrael does not have anything to shape their identity as a nation. Every nation is shaped by its *mazal*, which gives the nation its name, language, and writing style, among other things. Yisrael's identity is defined solely by their relationship with Hashem and their status as a holy nation. Their language is the holy tongue, which is the language of the Torah. Since Torah is the bond that holds the Jewish People together, those that defy the Torah and fail to act with holiness are set adrift without any meaning or common identity. Thus, as Rabbi Akiva said to Papus ben Yehudah, a Jew without the Torah is like a fish out of the water:[143] He can survive for a time but his eventual demise is assured.

Yisrael's status as the Chosen Nation grants them special privileges unavailable to any other nation, but when Yisrael betrays Hashem's Will, He hides His face from them and they are abandoned to their fate, without even a *mazal* to provide them with some level of protection. Consistent with this, the Torah compares Yisrael to both the stars of

---

140   *Ramban, Parashas Bo* 13:16.

141   *Maseches Sanhedrin* 37a.

142   *Kli Yakar, Parashas Vayeira* 22:17; *Maharsha, Chiddushei Aggados, Maseches Kesuvos* 66b.

143   *Maseches Berachos* 61b.

the heavens[144] and the dirt of the ground.[145] Yisrael, unlike other nations, lives only at the extremes — there is never a middle ground. Their status as privileged son of Hashem enables them to reach extraordinary heights, but at the same time the potential exists for a precipitous downfall. When the Jewish People achieve their purpose and are faithful to the will of Hashem, they reach heights beyond the reach of other nations — like the stars in the heavens. Conversely, when they throw off the yoke of the mitzvos, Hashem hides His face from them and they are reduced to the contemptible status of dirt that is trodden underfoot, an unfathomably low level below that of any other nation.

The Jewish nation's dual status is implied by the two names of Yaakov and Yisrael. Although Hashem changed Yaakov's name to Yisrael, the name Yaakov was left in place. The name Yaakov is derived from the word *eikev*, which means heel, and it describes the Jewish nation when they are downtrodden and underfoot. In contrast, the name Yisrael, related to the word *sar*, nobleman, describes the Jewish nation at their height. Importantly, however, even when the Jewish People are downtrodden, this condition is only temporary and they will eventually be restored to their previous glory.

---

144   *Parashas Vayeira* 22:18.
145   *Parashas Vayeitzei* 28:14.

THE SINS OF the generation of *Haflagah* set into motion a previous decree of Hashem that the people would be divided into seventy nations. At the same time, Avraham earned the merit of being the forefather of the seventy-first nation — the Jewish nation — which would be the only nation not under the *mazalos*. Unlike the other seventy nations, the occurrences of the Jewish nation are completely dependent on their merit and not on the *mazalos*.

AFTERWORD

After the sin of Adam and Chavah, the laws of nature were put into place, which made it more difficult to perceive the Divine Providence. The obscurity of Divine Providence eventually led to idolatry. However, in the period prior to the deluge, the Divine Presence became more apparent in the world and the earth began to produce in a way it had not done since before Adam sinned. This should have made it easier for the people to see the hand of Hashem. Indeed, it did accomplish this, but it had a downside as well; the great blessings the people experienced made them haughty and caused them to rebel against Hashem. Their sins made their continued existence untenable, and Hashem devastated the world with a deluge.

Noach and his family were the only survivors and they emerged from the ark into a vastly changed world. The deluge had weakened the earth and the cycle of the sun had changed. This ensured that the world would never again produce on the same scale as before. This new world was built upon the concept that one nation will become the focus of creation and all other nations would exist in its merit. After the sin of the generation of the *Haflagah* the people were divided into seventy nations, while a seventy-first nation, which had not yet come into existence, would became the focal point of Creation.

By virtue of his faith and deeds, Avraham was chosen to be the forefather of the seventy-first nation. His descendants would enjoy the fruits of Eretz Yisrael, the only land not devastated by the deluge. Avraham was not born into this role; to the contrary, he faced many challenges on his way to earning the distinction of becoming the forefather of Yisrael. Avraham managed to overcome every challenge and the merit that he accrued would stand by his descendants, who would ultimately become the Chosen Nation of Hashem.

AVRAHAM AVINU

GREAT IS MILAH BECAUSE THERE IS NO ONE WHO OCCUPIED HIMSELF IN TORAH AND MITZVOS LIKE AVRAHAM AND YET HE WAS ONLY CALLED "TAMIM" (WHOLE) FOR THE SAKE OF MILAH, AS THE TORAH STATES: "WALK IN FRONT OF ME AND BE TAMIM."

(MASECHES NEDARIM 32A)

INTRODUCTION TO STAGE III

The failure of the generation of the *Haflagah* to recognize Hashem underscored the contrast between them and Avram Ha'Ivri, so called because he stood on one side of the world, alone in his beliefs and actions, while everyone else in the world stood on the opposite side. Avram (his name before Hashem changed his name to Avraham) distinguished himself with His recognition of Hashem at the tender of age of three years old. This accomplishment is even more impressive considering the environment that Avram was raised in:

- The entire generation was steeped in idolatry and denial of Hashem.
- His father, Terach, peddled idols.[146]
- Nimrod pursued Avram and tried to kill him.[147]

Yet, already at an early age, Avram managed to defy the prevalent view of the independent power of the *mazalos* and stand firm in his belief in Divine Providence, with incredible self-sacrifice.

From all the people in the world, only Avram was fit to be chosen as the founding father of the future nation of Yisrael. There were other righteous people in the world, such as Shem ben Noach and Eiver, among others, but Avram was selected as the forefather of the nation who would receive the Torah, because he was the first to spread faith

---

146 *Bereishis Rabbah* 38:13.
147 Ibid.

in Hashem throughout the world.[148] While his contemporaries of the generation of the *Haflagah* prepared themselves for a "battle" against Hashem, Avram went from town to town and kingdom to kingdom teaching the people that there is One G-d who should be worshipped.[149]

In contrast to the prevalent view of the time, Avram proclaimed that Hashem is the sole power in the world[150] and that He had not abdicated His rule in any way. Avram recognized the hidden hand of Hashem orchestrating events behind the facade of nature. The Talmud relates that from the day Hashem created the world, no one called Hashem *Adon* until Avraham.[151] The term *Adon* indicates the dominion of Hashem over the works of nature. In particular, Avram attained unique insight into Divine Providence from the movements of the sun.

> *Avram said to himself, "How is it possible that the sun constantly cycles the earth without anyone causing it to move? It is impossible for it to move on its own!" He realized there is One G-d who moves the sun, and He created everything in the world, and there is no other G-d besides Him. He recognized that from the generation of Enosh, the entire world erred in their worshiping of the stars [from the erroneous belief that Hashem wanted them to worship His servants], until it came to the point where they completely forgot the truth [and they started believing that the sun and the stars were independent powers].[152]*

Avram's ability to correctly perceive Hashem's Presence in the world was the basis for his strong faith in the Creator. For these reasons, Avram was chosen to be the founder of the nation of Yisrael.

Upon the division of the people into nations and the selection of Avram as the forefather of the Chosen Nation, the world was

---

148   *Derash Moshe, Parashas Noach.*
149   *Rambam, Hilchos Avodas Kochavim* 1:3.
150   Rabbeinu Bachya, *Parashas Vayeira* 22:1.
151   *Maseches Berachos* 7b.
152   *Rambam, Hilchos Avodas Kochavim* 1:1–3.

transformed. If until now every person in the world was "chosen" and had an equal opportunity to achieve equal closeness with Hashem, henceforth only Avram and his descendants would have this privilege. Individuals among the nations who choose to convert and join the nation of Yisrael also gain this privileged status,[153] but all others are distanced from Hashem. However, every individual among the nations can earn merit even without converting to Judaism, by adhering to the Seven Noachide Laws. However, says the *Rambam*, he must do so only because Hashem commanded these mitzvos in the Torah and gave them to Moshe. Such a person is deemed to be from the *chassidei umos ha'olam* — righteous among the nations, and merits a share in the World to Come.[154]

However, the merit that a non-Jew earns by keeping the Noachide Laws is negligible compared to the merit that a Jewish person earns by keeping the 613 mitzvos of the Torah, as the Talmud tells us: "Hashem wanted to bring merit to Yisrael and therefore He gave them an abundance of Torah and mitzvos."[155] The Torah could not yet be given until the descendants of Avraham were sufficiently numerous to become a nation. In the meantime, Avraham and his descendants were given individual mitzvos as part of the process of their transformation into the Chosen Nation of Hashem. This process would occur in several stages. Each of the forefathers, starting with Avraham, would move Yisrael one step closer to its destiny and the fulfillment of Hashem's original intention in the Creation of the world.

---

153   Avraham is the father of all converts to Judaism in the same way that he is the father of the nation of Yisrael (*Maseches Chagigah* 3a).

154   *Rambam, Hilchos Melachim* 8:11.

155   *Maseches Makos* 23b.

TEN

REBIRTH

The Talmud states: "The first two thousand years of the world were the era of emptiness, while the next two thousand years were the years of Torah. The two thousand years of Torah began when Avram, at fifty-two years old, took upon himself the mission of spreading belief in Hashem and His Torah among his contemporaries, as the *Targum* states, "And the souls that [Avram and Sarai] committed to the Torah."[156]

By bringing the light of Torah to the world, Avraham became the spiritual father of the world. This is consistent with the statement of the sages that "anyone who teaches the son of his friend Torah is regarded as if he raised him."[157] Avraham brought Torah to the entire world and thus was considered to be its father, as we will see.

The *Abarbanel* maintains that Hashem created the world three times:[158]

- The world was initially created with Adam and Chavah.
- It was created again with Noach and his three sons after the devastation of the Great Flood.
- It was recreated again when Avraham became the founding father of the world.

---

156   *Maseches Avodah Zarah* 9a, and *Rashi.*
157   *Maseches Sanhedrin* 19b.
158   Beginning of *Parashas Lech Lecha.*

The world that Avraham lived in did not undergo any significant physical changes, yet he initiated a new world in a spiritual sense — the new world of the Torah. The prophet Yeshayah therefore refers to Avraham as Adam,[159] because he was the spiritual father of the world, much as Adam was the physical father of the world. Likewise, Avraham's wife Sarah is considered the spiritual mother of the world.[160]

Considering that Avraham initiated a new world, we gain insight into Hashem's promise to him that he would have children. Avram said to Hashem, "Behold, to me You have not given children and behold, my [servant] will inherit me."[161] Avram doubted his ability to have children because he saw in the stars that he would be barren. Although the Jewish People as a nation are not under a specific *mazal*, an individual Jewish person *is* subject to the influence of the *mazalos*.[162] This is especially true with regard to fertility, longevity, and livelihood.[163]

The Torah states that Hashem lifted Avram above the stars to show him how He would alter the *mazalos* for his sake.[164] Hashem said to Avram, "Why do you think [you will not have children], because the star 'tzeddek' is in the west (which does not allow for him to have children — *Rashi*)? I will place it in the east!"[165] The repositioning of the *mazalos* would allow Avram to have children.

Despite this, we find that changing the position of the star *tzeddek* was not sufficient, a change of name was also required. Hashem said, "Take leave of your astrology; you see in the stars that you will not have children. Avram will not have children, but Avraham will have children, Sarai will not give birth, but Sarah will give birth."[166] Hashem

---

159 Chazal teach us that the phrase *"ha'adam ha'gadol b'anakim"* (*Yehoshua* 14:15) is a reference to Avraham.
160 *Shelah, Parashas Chayei Sarah.*
161 *Parashas Lech Lecha* 15:3.
162 Rabbeinu Bachya, *Parashas Eikev* 8:18.
163 *Maseches Mo'ed Katan* 28a.
164 *Parashas Lech Lecha* 15:5.
165 *Maseches Shabbos* 156b.
166 *Rashi, Parashas Lech Lecha* 15:5.

promised Avram that a change in their names would effect a change in their *mazal*.

Why was a name change necessary considering that Hashem repositioned the *mazalos* in a way that would allow them to have children?

The answer is that the name change allowed for the repositioning of the *mazalos*. The Talmud declares that a reconfiguration of the *mazalos* cannot occur without a new creation of the world.[167] Thus it was necessary to add the letter *hei* to the names of Avram and Sarai. Hashem created the world with the letter *hei*, and with the addition of that letter to the names of Avram and Sarai, the world was in fact being created anew. The new world of Torah was ushered in and a reconfiguration of the *mazalos* was now possible.[168]

The new names of Avraham and Sarah signified a monumental transformation in their standing. It was not just a mere modification of title; it symbolized their pioneering status in the new world of Torah. They were no longer mere individuals, but had been converted into something much bigger:

- The new name of Avraham was an acronym for *av hamon goyim* — father of a multitude of nations — as Avraham was regarded as the forefather of the entire world.[169]
- Sarai's new name of Sarah signified the same concept. The name Sarai means "my princess," while her new name Sarah signified that she was the princess over all,[170] as Sarah was the mother of the new world of Torah.

---

167 *Maseches Taanis* 28a.

168 Rabbeinu Bachya, *Parashas Toldos* 25:21 and *Parashas Vayeitzei* 29:35. Rabbeinu Bachya maintains that Rachel suggested to Yaakov that the reason she was unable to conceive was because she didn't have the letter *hei* in her name, unlike the other wives of Yaakov. To address this, she gave Yaakov her maidservant Bilhah for a wife so that she will "build from her." Considering that the letter *hei* appears twice in Bilhah's name, Rachel was suggesting that she would build from the second *hei* in Bilhah's name, as Bilhah would use one *hei* and Rachel would use the other.

169 *Parashas Lech Lecha* 17:5.

170 *Rashi*, ibid.

We see that while Avraham and Sarah were not parents of the world in a physical sense, they were so in a spiritual sense. Upon the inauguration of the new world, the realities of the previous world were no longer relevant. Although previously the *mazalos* did not allow for Avram and Sarai to have children, the new world ushered in by the reconfiguration of the *mazalos* brought in a new reality. The star *tzeddek* that had previously been in the west was now in the east, which allowed for Avraham and Sarah to have children.

The generations prior to Avraham were spiritually bereft and devoid of Torah. Everything prior to him was darkness. Avraham's lifetime was the dawn of a meaningful new world; the new world of Torah. It was fitting that Avraham was born in Kasdim,[171] the darkest of all nations, a nation that Hashem said He "regrets" having created.[172] This is the concept of darkness before dawn — the darkest part of the night is the period right before dawn. Avraham emerged from the utmost darkness of the land of Kasdim, and he shone forth like the bright light of dawn.[173]

Since Avraham initiated a meaningful fresh start of the world, he was disconnected from the previous generations. Consistent with this, the midrash states: Hashem said to Avraham, "I am dismissing you from honoring your father, but I am not dismissing anyone else. Not only that, but I will precede his death to your departure [to Eretz Canaan]." [174] The *Maharal* explains: Avraham was exempt from the mitzvah of honoring his father because he was disconnected from his parents. Avraham was the light of the world, while the generations prior to Avraham, including his father, Terach, lived in an era of

---

171   Hashem said to Avraham: "I am Hashem who took you out of Ur Kasdim" (*Parashas Lech Lecha* 15:7). However, the *Ramban* maintains that Avraham Avinu was born in Charan and only later went with his father to the nation of Kasdim. The *Maharal* disputes this because the Talmud states (*Maseches Pesachim* 87b) that when Hashem exiled the Jewish nation to Babylon, they were being sent to the house of their mother, which implies that their origins are in Babylon, which is Kasdim (*Sefer Gevuras Hashem, perek* 5).

172   *Maseches Sukkah* 52b.

173   *Gur Aryeh, Sefer Gevuras Hashem, perek* 5.

174   *Bereishis Rabbah, Parashas Lech Lecha*.

darkness. There is no connection between light and darkness, because the arrival of light chases away the darkness; similarly, the light of Avraham dissipated the darkness of Terach.[175] Thus, although Terach was the biological father of Avraham, in a spiritual sense he was a stranger to Avraham.[176]

The death of Terach is mentioned in the Torah at the very end of *Parashas Noach*, prior to the beginning of the Torah's narrative of Avraham. Terach lived for many years after Avraham's departure from Charan, yet the Torah chronicles his death prior to any mention of this. This is because when a new structure is built, the rubble from the previous structure is cleared away to make room for the new. Avraham was the cornerstone of the new world and his life was the start of a new existence. The rubble of the previous generations had to be cleared away before Avraham's new foundation could be built. Although Terach was Avraham's father, he was from the previous generation of emptiness, and any mention of him had to be cleared out of the way before the Torah could embark on the narrative of Avraham and his departure from Charan.[177]

---

175 Although Terach repented from his bad ways, he only did so right before his death (*Ramban, Parashas Noach* 11:32).

176 Likewise, Yaakov and the *Shevatim* are not considered to be descendants of their evil forefathers, Besuel and Lavan. All of the forefathers, not just Avraham, are considered to be *av hamon goyim* and represent a new beginning (*Netziv, Sefer Ha'amek Davar* in *Harchev Davar, Parashas Lech Lecha* 17:4). The Dubno Maggid explains that the reason that our forefathers and mothers were barren — with the exception of Yitzchak and Yaakov — was so that their children would not be considered their natural, biological progeny and would not be considered to have descended from the previous wicked generations (*Sefer Kochav MiYaakov*).

177 This explains why the account in the Torah of Avraham starts with the command of Hashem, "You shall go from your land, from your place of birth and your father's house to the land that I will show you" (*Parashas Lech Lecha* 12:1). The very first command of Hashem is that he shall depart from his family and his place of birth. His destination was not as important as the departure from his family and starting a new life, therefore the Torah does not mention his destination right away. Even without any important destination, his departure was purpose in itself because he had to disconnect himself from his family and set out on his own so that the world could start anew.

AVRAM AND SARAI emerged from a world of darkness and brought the light of the Torah to the world. Their new names of Avraham and Sarah signified their new status as the forefather and foremother of the world. Their new status brought in a new *mazal* and a new reality, which allowed them to have a son, Yitzchak, who would carry on their legacy.

ELEVEN

THE KOHEN: PARADIGM OF EMUNAH

The midrash states that Avraham inherited this world and the next world as a reward for his faith.[178] It was the greatness of his faith that set Avraham apart from everyone who preceded him and made him the founding father of the world. Avraham was called a *tzur*, a rock, because his strength of faith was the foundation stone of the world.[179] However, faith — by its nature — is an internal trait that is not evident on the outside. For Avraham to fulfill his public role, it was important for his faith to be revealed to all so that it would be obvious why he was chosen from all others. Therefore, Avraham, and the strength of his faith, was tested ten times, as the Mishnah teaches: "Avraham was tested ten times and he passed all of them to show how beloved was Avraham."[180] After the final test, the test of the *Akeidah*, Hashem said to him, "Now I have what to respond to the Satan and the nations of the world who wonder why you are so beloved to me."[181] It was now apparent to all that Avraham truly deserved to be the forefather of Yisrael.[182]

As we said, Avraham's great faith was predicated on his ability to perceive the Presence of Hashem in all the occurrences of the world.

178　*Shemos Rabbah, perek* 22.
179　*Sefer Yeshayah* 51:1. See also *Radak* and *Ibn Ezra*.
180　*Pirkei Avos* 5:3.
181　*Rashi, Parashas Vayeira* 22:12.
182　*Maharal, Sefer Gevuras Hashem, perek* 7, *Sefer Derech Chaim* 5:3.

Avraham saw nature for what it truly is: a facade that Hashem put in place to mask His Presence in the world. How did Avraham manage to perceive what other people of his generation could not? Avraham's perception of Hashem's Presence was due to his exceedingly humble nature. It is not only nature that interferes with our perception of the Presence of Hashem, but also an inflated sense of self, which blocks us from seeing what should be obvious — the hand of Hashem orchestrating events in this world. Avraham's remarkable humility allowed him to look beyond his own self and experience the Divine Presence in the world.

This can be seen from Avraham's fifth test when he went out to battle with the four kings, despite the seemingly impossible odds.[183] Avraham was at a great numerical disadvantage; he had a scant 318 people on his side against four powerful kings and their armies, who had already proven their mettle when they vanquished the armies of the five kings.[184] Avraham and his people lacked even the most basic weapons; they were forced to resort to throwing dirt and straw at the enemy.[185] Although victory seemed impossible, Avraham nevertheless put his faith in Hashem and he waged battle with the four kings. With Hashem at his side, Avraham and his people prevailed; the dirt miraculously turned into swords and the straw turned into arrows.[186] Through these miracles, Avraham and his people managed to vanquish the enemy and rescue Lot from captivity.

Tellingly, Avraham did not attribute his success in battle to his own might; to the contrary, he attributed his victory solely to Hashem. Avraham commented about his victory, "I am but dirt and ashes."[187] *Rashi* explains, "I should have been dirt at the hands of the Four Kings and ashes at the hands of Nimrod if not for Your mercy that stood by

---

183 *Bartenura, Pirkei Avos* 5:3.
184 According to Rabbeinu Bachya, Avraham actually fought with only Eliezer at his side, as the numerical value of Eliezer is 318.
185 *Maseches Taanis* 21a.
186 *Maseches Sanhedrin* 108b.
187 *Parashas Vayeira* 18:27.

me."[188] Avraham believed that his victory over the four kings was due to Hashem's mercy, not because he was a great warrior. He felt he was unworthy of the miracles that he experienced because, in his mind, he had already been rewarded for the mitzvos he had done and no reward would be awaiting him in the next world. [189] Even though the miracles he experienced were an outcome of his self-sacrifice to sanctify the Name of Hashem, Avraham felt that his survival was sufficient reward for his righteousness. It was this humility and self-effacement that gave Avraham the ability to look beyond his own self and recognize Hashem's hand orchestrating events behind the facade of nature.

After Avraham defeated the four kings, Shem, the son of Noach, who was the High Priest of Hashem,[190] recited the blessing: "Blessed is Avraham to the G-d on High, the Maker of heaven and earth."[191] Shem erred by blessing Avraham prior to blessing Hashem, and as a consequence, the priesthood was taken away from him and was given instead to Avraham.[192]

Why did Shem bless Avraham prior to blessing Hashem? Shem was granted the title High Priest of Hashem because of his righteous and G-d-fearing ways, and certainly he did not believe that the blessing of Avraham took precedence over the blessing of Hashem! The *Maharal* explains that Shem reached an awareness of Hashem's greatness by observing Divine Providence in the world and the miracles Hashem does for those who love and fear Him. By witnessing the great miracles that Avraham experienced in his battle with the four kings, Shem achieved greater heights in his awareness of Divine Providence. His blessing of Avraham reflected the new heights in faith he had achieved, and thus this blessing was essentially a blessing of Hashem.[193]

If Shem blessed Avraham prior to blessing Hashem because Avraham helped him achieve greater faith in Hashem, why was he punished with the forfeiture of his priesthood?

---

188   *Rashi, ibid.*
189   *Rashi, Parashas Lech Lecha 15:1; Yalkut.*
190   *Parashas Noach 14:18 and Rashi.*
191   *Parashas Lech Lecha 14:19.*
192   *Maseches Nedarim 32b.*
193   *Maharal, Chiddushei Aggados, ibid.*

Shem's loss of the priesthood was not a punishment, but rather an inevitable outcome of the fact that Avraham was more deserving of the priesthood than Shem. Shem's blessing of Avraham made it apparent that he had not achieved full cognizance of the hidden hand of Hashem orchestrating nature. For one who sees nature as no more than a facade hiding Hashem's Presence there is no difference between the natural and the supernatural; nature is just as much a miracle as a supernatural event. Since the miracles that occurred for Avraham helped Shem reach a greater level of faith in Hashem, it is apparent that Shem viewed nature and the supernatural differently.

In contrast, Avraham did not need to witness great miracles to perceive the hand of Hashem in the world, because he saw Hashem's hand "through" the facade of nature. Avraham's more advanced perception of the Presence of Hashem in the world made him a better fit for the priesthood than Shem, and therefore Shem was forced to cede his position as High Priest to Avraham.

AVRAHAM'S CLARITY OF faith allowed him to see through the facade of nature and to experience nature as a supernatural event in the same way that others experience open miracles. Avraham's advanced perception of the Divine Presence made him worthy of being the High Priest. Avraham took over the priesthood from Shem who had been the High Priest until then.

TWELVE

THE MITZVAH OF BRIS MILAH

Following his attainment of the priesthood upon the defeat of the four kings, Avraham was tested with the mitzvah of *bris milah*, the sixth of his Ten Tests.[194] Avraham voluntarily kept all the mitzvos of the Torah, even the mitzvos that had yet to be established. Avraham's keen perception of the Divine Presence gave him the ability to perceive the mitzvos with his own wisdom, even without having heard them from Hashem. Aside from the Seven Noachide Laws, Hashem commanded Avraham in one special mitzvah — the mitzvah of *bris milah*. This mitzvah was the eighth mitzvah that Avraham was commanded to do, and it was to be performed on the eighth day of a boy's life. The mitzvah of *bris milah* is associated with the number eight because the number seven represents the natural order of the world that was created in seven days, while the number eight symbolizes transcendence over nature. The *bris milah* that is performed on the eighth day is beyond nature, as it elevates and refines the human body that was created during the seven days of Creation. By performing the mitzvah of *bris milah*, man elevates himself above the natural order of the world and brings himself close to Hashem.

Unlike Avraham, Adam HaRishon was born without a foreskin, and he did not need a *bris milah*. This indicated that Adam was born with a great degree of sanctity. Only one who has a *bris milah* has full

---

194 Rabbeinu Yonah, *Pirkei Avos* 5:3.

control over all the limbs of his body, which is the essence of sanctity.[195] When Adam sinned, his *milah* was covered up, which means that he no longer had full control over his limbs and thus lost some of his original sanctity.

In contrast to Adam, Avraham was born on a very low spiritual level. Avraham's ascent to the heights of spiritual achievement occurred at a slow-moving pace, one small step at a time. Rav Pinchas Horowitz maintains that it took Avraham forty-nine years to climb his way out of the forty-nine levels of impurity that he had been born into.[196] It then took him another forty-nine years to climb up to the forty-ninth level of spiritual purity. Hashem commanded Avraham in the mitzvah of *bris milah* only after he reached the forty-ninth level of spiritual purity. The forty-ninth level of sanctity, which equals seven times seven, is one step below the sanctity of the *bris milah*, which is symbolized by the number eight. Thus, it took Avraham ninety-nine years to reach the sanctity that Adam HaRishon was born into.

Yet, Avraham managed to maintain and increase his sanctity while Adam HaRishon suffered a decline in his sanctity. Why was Avraham, who was born with such a low degree of sanctity able to accomplish what Adam could not maintain? The answer is twofold:

- Adam was born with the sanctity of the *bris milah*, while Avraham worked long and hard to reach that level of sanctity.
- Avraham endured tremendous self-sacrifice to perform the mitzvah of *bris milah*. A mitzvah that is done with self-sacrifice endures.

As we said, Avraham was born in the darkness of Kasdim and he started his life on a low spiritual level. He climbed toward spiritual purity in slow and steady steps, before finally reaching the summit of sanctity. Sanctity that is accomplished with much toil is enduring because it is very dear to a person and he does not give it up easily.

---

195   *Maseches Nedarim* 32b.
196   *Panim Yafos, Parashas Lech Lecha.*

The spirituality that Avraham achieved with the mitzvah of *bris milah* endured for another reason as well: the self-sacrifice that Avraham endured in the process of fulfilling this mitzvah. Avraham's detractors attempted to prevent him from performing the mitzvah, as the Torah relates that Avraham did the *bris milah* in middle of the day in defiance of the people of the generation who threated to prevent him.[197]

Moreover, Avraham willingly went ahead with the *bris milah* despite his fear that it would kill him. Avraham performed the mitzvah on his family members before doing so on himself because he was afraid he would not survive the mitzvah. This fear was not unfounded; the *Peirush Rosh* says that Avraham did the mitzvah of *bris milah* on many children prior to his own *bris milah* and all of the children died; thus there was a real concern that Avraham, who was already ninety-nine years old, would also die from the *bris milah*.[198] In addition, there was a concern that Avraham in his weakened state would be vulnerable to a revenge attack from the relatives of the four kings who were killed by his hands.[199] Despite his fear of death, and despite his detractors, Avraham went ahead with the mitzvah. This self-sacrifice made the mitzvah enduring.

We can understand why the sanctity of *bris milah* was enduring for Avraham for the reasons stated above, but why is this true for his descendants? The Torah commands us to perform the mitzvah of *bris milah* on a newborn at the age of eight days. Why doesn't the Torah have us delay performing the *bris milah* to give the newborn time to work his way up to sanctity and allow the mitzvah to be earned?

This is actually not necessary, because as a legacy of their descendancy from Avraham, the sanctity of the mitzvah of *bris milah* has become an ingrained hereditary trait. This can be seen from the Mishnah that teaches us that all Jewish People are called *mulim* (circumcised), even those who are in reality uncircumcised![200] The *Maharal* explains that the Jewish People are characterized by their inborn trait of sanctity

---

197 *Parashas Lech Lecha* 17:23, and *Rashi*.
198 *Peirush HaRosh, Parashas Lech Lecha* 17:13.
199 Rav Yonasan Eibshitz.
200 *Sefer Netzach Yisrael, perek* 6.

and even those who have not actually undergone a *bris milah* are not excluded from this.[201]

What's more, the precedent that Avraham set by putting his life in danger for the mitzvah of *bris milah* became an enduring legacy for the Jewish People throughout the generations. The degree to which the Jewish people have sacrificed for the mitzvah of *bris milah* exceeds that of other mitzvos. The Talmud teaches us: "Any mitzvah for which Yisrael has been willing to give up their life at a time of persecution, such as *avodah zarah* and *milah* remains strong in their hands."[202] Likewise, David HaMelech said,[203] "Because for You we are being slaughtered all of the days." The midrash explains: "This is a reference to the mitzvah of *bris milah*, which has been the cause of many deaths over the years."[204] The self-sacrifice that the Jewish People demonstrated for the mitzvah of *bris milah* is a legacy from our forefather Avraham.

Bris milah is more than just a mitzvah: it is the symbol of Avraham's covenant with Hashem. Hashem established an everlasting covenant with Avraham and his descendants when He said, "And I shall give my covenant between Me and you."[205] When we perform the mitzvah of *bris milah* we recite the blessing of "to enter into the covenant of Avraham," because when we perform the mitzvah we are undergoing the same covenant that Avraham underwent.

At the time of the *Haflagah*, Hashem selected Avraham to be the forefather of the Chosen Nation; however, He had not yet made a covenant with him. When Avraham was given the mitzvah of *bris milah*, the covenant was renewed with him, with the *bris milah* serving as the sign of the covenant. Avraham willingly accepted the covenant upon himself when he "fell on his face."[206] This acceptance implied a commitment to cast aside his own will and to consider only the will of Hashem.

---

201   *Sefer Netzach Yisrael, perek* 6.
202   *Maseches Shabbos* 130a.
203   *Sefer Tehillim* 44.
204   *Yalkut Shimoni* §837.
205   *Parashas Lech Lecha* 17:2.
206   Ibid. 17:3.

Rav Shimshon Raphael Hirsch explains that by falling on his face, Avraham was demonstrating his willingness to enter into the covenant of Hashem, because in such a position, he could no longer see, but only listen, which indicated that he was giving up his independence entirely. This is similar to the angels in front of Hashem's throne, who have their faces and feet covered with their wings, an indication that they are prepared to use their powers of flight to carry out the commands of Hashem. By accepting the covenant, Avraham agreed to put aside his own will, and from then on to only consider the will of Hashem. This was the precursor of the future statement of "We will do and we will hear" that was uttered by his descendants at *Matan Torah*, which conveyed the same sentiment — that they were prepared to put aside their own will for the will of Hashem.

THE BRIS MILAH was one of the ten tests that Avraham faced, but this mitzvah was much more than just a test: it symbolized the covenant between Hashem and Avraham. The sanctity and self-sacrifice that is inherent in this mitzvah would be an enduring legacy for Avraham and his descendants.

THIRTEEN

THE AKEIDAH

The commitment that Avraham made to faithfully follow the will of Hashem was eventually put to the ultimate test — the test of the *Akeidah*. This test was the tenth and final test that Avraham faced, and passing this test would seal his role as the forefather of Yisrael. Hashem commanded Avraham, "Please take your son, your only one, the one that you love, Yitzchak, and go to the land of Moriah and bring him there as an *olah* sacrifice on one of the mountains that I shall tell you."[207] The test of the *Akeidah* was the culmination of Avraham's ten tests,[208] and it was the pinnacle of all of Avraham's achievements in his faith in Hashem. The commandment of Hashem to bring his son as a sacrifice was unfathomably challenging, not only because of the obvious difficulty of relinquishing his long-awaited and much-beloved son, but also because the practice of human sacrifice was something that Avraham had always condemned.

Rav Chaim Shmuelevitz explains[209] that the primary test that Avraham faced was not giving up the life of his son — as difficult as that was — but being forced to repudiate his entire life's work. Avraham had repeatedly preached the importance of distancing oneself from idolatry and worshipping the one and only G-d. Now that Avraham was

---

207 *Parashas Vayeira* 22:2.

208 The *Rambam* maintains that the *Akeidah* was the tenth test (*Peirush Mishnayos, Maseches Avos* 5:4). However, Rabbeinu Yonah maintains that it was the ninth test.

209 *Maamar Eved Hashem, Alef Ki Sisa* 5732.

bringing his own child as a sacrifice, the people were certain to believe that he engaged in idolatry (as this was the practice of idol worshippers). Avraham was sure to be dismissed as a hypocrite, which would prevent him from continuing his mission to spread belief in Hashem throughout the world. He could have interpreted Hashem's command in such a way that would have exonerated him from actually bringing Yitzchak as a sacrifice, yet Avraham fought off all temptations to apply human reasoning to the commandment of Hashem and he proceeded without reservations. Avraham went as a servant carrying out the will of his Master, without any qualms or misgivings.[210]

Furthermore, says the *Malbim*, Avraham had achieved great insight into the ways of Hashem, and he was able to determine with absolute certainty that the act of human sacrifice, and especially the slaughtering of one's own son, was abhorrent to Hashem. Nevertheless, through his great faith and love of Hashem, he overcame all misgivings, and pressed forth in his quest to fulfill the command of Hashem.[211]

The trial of the *Akeidah* was a test of Yitzchak's faith as well.[212] Yitzchak was aware that his father Avraham intended to bring him as a sacrifice, but nonetheless, he went along willingly.[213] According to the *Chasam Sofer*, the test that Yitzchak faced was in some ways more difficult than Avraham's. Avraham heard the commandment of the *Akeidah* directly from Hashem, while Yitzchak only heard it from a prophet — his father Avraham. The commandment to sacrifice his son contradicted Avraham's previous understanding of Hashem's will, but since he heard Hashem command him to do so, it was less challenging to push aside his previous understanding of human sacrifice in favor of Hashem's explicit commandment.[214]

---

210 *Avi Ezri, Hilchos Yesodei Torah* 7:6, and ibid.
211 *Malbim, Parashas Bereishis* 22:5.
212 All of our forefathers were tested, not just Avraham (*Maseches Sanhedrin* 107; *Bereishis Rabbah* 15).
213 *Rashi, Parashas Vayeira* 22:8.
214 The *Chasam Sofer* points out that in other ways the test was more difficult for Avraham than it was for Yitzchak because Avraham had three days to think it over and he nevertheless went ahead with it, while Yitzchak did not know at first that he was being brought as a *korban* (*Sefer Toras Moshe Parashas Vayeira* 22:4).

Yitzchak had achieved the same degree of wisdom as Avraham and thus was equally aware of the abhorrence of human sacrifice.[215] Since he did not hear the commandment directly from Hashem, it would have been reasonable for Yitzchak to doubt the veracity of his father's prophecy, rather than admit that he had erred in his previous view. It was a formidable challenge for Yitzchak to subordinate himself to the prophecy of Avraham despite the contradiction to his previous beliefs. Yitzchak managed to overcome this challenge and he put his complete faith in Avraham's prophecy, even though it would have resulted in his death. Father and son went happily together, each secure in the knowledge that Hashem had commanded this sacrifice and therefore it must be the right thing to do.[216]

With this understanding, the test of the *Akeidah* was comparable to the test that Adam HaRishon faced with the *mitzvah* of the *Eitz HaDaas*:

- Adam perceived the spiritual qualities of the fruit of the *Eitz HaDaas* and understood that partaking from it would uplift him spiritually. It seemed reasonable to him that Hashem was not actually prohibiting the Tree of Knowledge, but warning him of the consequences of eating from it.

- Likewise, Avraham was aware that human sacrifice was abhorrent to Hashem and would distance him from Hashem. It seemed logical to interpret the commandment in a nonliteral way and spare himself from the gut-wrenching act of bringing his son as a sacrifice. But Avraham fought off this temptation

---

215   Yitzchak did not reach this understanding because he was taught by his father Avraham; he attained his wisdom on his own. Yitzchak achieved Torah wisdom and great spiritual heights independently of Avraham. *Rashi* writes that each one of the forefathers was independently worthy of a covenant with Hashem without the merit of the others (*Parashas Bechukosai* 26:42). Thus, when Avraham informed Yitzchak that it was the will of Hashem that he be brought as a sacrifice, this was not easy for him to accept. If Avraham had been the source of all of his wisdom, it would have been less of a challenge for him to go along with it, since his teacher was retracting his teachings and informing him that he erred. However, since Avraham was not his teacher, it was difficult for Yitzchak to accept the prophecy of Avraham, which challenged the wisdom that he had attained (*Teshuvos Chasam Sofer, Orach Chaim* §20).

216   *Teshuvos Chasam Sofer, Orach Chaim* §208.

because he knew that human calculations must be pushed aside when confronted with a Divine commandment.

The similarities continue: As we saw, Hashem never intended that Adam abstain forever from the *Eitz HaDaas*. He only wanted Adam to demonstrate his loyalty to his Creator by abstaining until the onset of Shabbos.[217] Through the power of Adam's faith, demonstrated by his adherence to the word of Hashem, the *Eitz HaDaas* would have become an object of a mitzvah upon the onset of Shabbos. At that time Adam would have made Kiddush on its juice. Similarly, Hashem never intended for Yitzchak to be brought as a sacrifice, but only that Avraham exhibit his faith in Hashem by placing him on the altar and binding his arms and legs.

Thus, says the *Chasam Sofer*, upon passing the test of the *Akeidah*, Avraham rectified the sin of Adam HaRishon.[218]

The test of the *Akeidah* atoned for the sin of Chavah as well: Chavah did not hear the prohibition of eating from the *Eitz HaDaas* directly from Hashem, but rather, from her husband, Adam, and she was obligated to heed his words. Her failure to do so demonstrated a lack of faith in Adam as the emissary of Hashem. This failure was corrected by Yitzchak, who demonstrated his faith in his father Avraham as an emissary of Hashem, when he obeyed Avraham's instructions and went willingly to the *Akeidah*. The faith of Yitzchak sowed the seeds for the future acceptance by his descendants of Moshe's role as an emissary of Hashem, when they willingly accepted the Torah taught to them by Moshe.[219]

Following the *Akeidah*, Hashem swore to Avraham, "I will bless you and multiply your descendants like the stars of the heaven and like the sand at the edge of the sea, and your descendants will inherit the gates of their enemies."[220] The *Ramban* explains that although this

---

217 Rabbi Moshe Chaim Luzzatto, *Daas Tevunos*; *Chasam Sofer, Sefer Toras Moshe, Parashas Bereishis*.

218 *Shelah*, see *Bereishis Rabbah* 14:6.

219 Rav Shimshon Raphael Hirsch, *Parashas Vayeira* 22:3. The Written Torah was heard directly from Hashem, as the entire Torah is included in the Ten Commandments (*Rashi, Parashas Mishpatim* 24:12).

220 *Parashas Vayeira* 22:18.

had already been promised to Avraham,[221] it was now sealed with an ironclad guarantee. Hashem swore with His Great Name that even if Avraham's descendants sin, it would not result in their extinction or in their extermination at the hands of their enemies.[222] Avraham was now assured of the eternity of his legacy; no occurrence could ever alter the reality of his descendants as the Chosen Nation.

With his legacy assured, Avraham was elevated above all other people. Rav Shimshon Raphael Hirsch elaborates: Avraham's success in heeding the command of Hashem, even when it was contrary to everything he believed, elevated him above all the people in the world and proved he was no longer in the category of a *ben Noach*. When Avraham reached the place of the *Akeidah* he said to his traveling companions, "You sit here with the donkey, and I and the lad will go."[223] Here, at the foot of Mount Moriah was the parting between the descendants of Avraham and the B'nei Noach. Up until they reached Mount Moriah, they could go together because B'nei Noach are also children of G-d, but a *ben Noach* can only reach the foot of the mountain; he cannot scale its heights. Only a Yisrael can give himself up to the will of G-d, in angel-like fashion, to cover up eye and foot and cheerfully and courageously use his powers to soar upward in his fulfillment of the will of G-d. It is this commitment to Hashem's will that separates a Yisrael from a *ben Noach*. A Yisrael puts aside his own judgment in favor of the Divine judgment; he does not consider his own will but instead faithfully follows the will of Hashem. For a Yisrael, the criterion for a "good" act is the will of Hashem; an act may seem bad or even cruel, but if it was commanded by Hashem, it is "good."[224]

With the passage of all ten tests, Avraham and his future descendants would henceforth be regarded as distinct and superior to all other people, as the Talmud states: "You (Yisrael) are called Adam, but [the

---

221   *Parashas Lech Lecha* 13:16, 15:5.
222   *Ramban, Parashas Vayeira* 22:18.
223   Ibid.
224   Rav Shimshon Raphael Hirsch, *Parashas Vayeira* 22:5, 11. However, after *Matan Torah* even a *ben Noach* is obligated to perform the Noachide Laws because Hashem commanded them, and not because he deems it to be the right thing to do (*Rambam, Hilchos Melachim* 8:11).

non-Jewish nations] are not called Adam."[225] The *Maharal* explains that Yisrael is referred to as "Adam" because their superiority over the other nations is similar to the superiority that Adam had over all other creatures.[226] Whereas previously, there were four levels of beings in the world (inanimate, plant, animal, and human), now there was a fifth level — Yisrael.[227] Yisrael stands alone as the only nation directly under Hashem's Providence and not under any intermediary. This special connection with Hashem elevates them above all the nations of the world and puts them into a category of their own.

The unique status of Yisrael is not only when they act in a manner that is consistent with their status as sons of Hashem, but even when they act contrary to His will, and even when they engage in idolatry.[228] Thus, when Hashem chose Yisrael it made them eternally chosen. Nothing can ever cause the connection to be severed or even weakened.

Still, Yisrael's status as the Chosen Nation does not mean that all others have been completely rejected. All people of the world can make themselves into sons of Hashem by submitting to His will and performing the Noachide Laws. However, there will always be a distinction between the Jewish People and other nations. B'nei Yisrael are not merely sons of Hashem, but the *bechor* (firstborn son) of Hashem. One can have many children, but he can only have one *bechor*. The status of the *bechor* is unassailable, no other son can ever become a *bechor* regardless of how many sons are born after him; likewise, B'nei Yisrael will never lose their status as the Chosen Nation of Hashem.

---

225 *Maseches Bava Metzia*, 114b.
226 *Maharal, Sefer Gur Aryeh, Parashas Bereishis* 1:1, *Parashas Vayigash* 46:10.
227 *Sefer HaKuzari* 2:44.
228 *Maseches Kiddushin* 36a.

THE AKEIDAH WAS the tenth and final test that Avraham faced and the pinnacle of his achievements. The *Akeidah* was a test for Yitzchak as well, with regard to his faith in his father as an emissary of Hashem. Father and son went happily to the *Akeidah* secure in their knowledge that they were performing the will of Hashem despite their inability to comprehend it.

AFTERWORD

With his remarkable faith, Avraham ushered in the dawn of a new world and accomplished what Adam had not: His faith in Hashem held fast and did not waiver even when confronted with overwhelming challenges to everything he held dear. Avraham's achievements were even more remarkable in light of the fact that he stood alone in his faith in Hashem, in defiance of the universal belief of the times, which denied Divine Providence.

Together with his son, Yitzchak, Avraham rectified the sin of Adam and Chavah and made the world fit for the giving of the Torah. The Torah had not been given to Adam because his sin of eating from the *Eitz HaDaas* proved him unworthy of it. By overcoming their misgivings on the way to the *Akeidah*, Avraham and Yitzchak demonstrated the purity of faith necessary for the acceptance of the Torah. They paved the way for their descendants to proclaim the ultimate demonstration of faith: "We will hear and we will do."[229]

Nevertheless, the Torah was not given to Avraham. The Torah would only be given to the Jewish People as a nation, and not to an individual, even to one as great as Avraham. The nation of Yisrael was founded not only on the spiritual strength of Avraham, but also on that of Yitzchak and Yaakov. Each one of the forefathers contributed his own unique spiritual characteristics to the future Jewish nation. The Talmud tells

---

229 *Parashas Va'eschanan* 5:24.

us that there is a special spiritual strength in the number three:[230] a three-stranded rope is not easily frayed.[231] The spiritual strengths of our three forefathers complemented each other and provided a deep spiritual foundation for their descendants.

---

230   *Maseches Kesuvos* 62b.
231   *Sefer Koheles* 4:12.

YAAKOV
AND EISAV

"And the children grew." Rabbi Levi says,
"This can be compared to a myrtle tree
and a thorn bush that are growing on top
of each other, and when they grow and
spread out, one gives off a fragrance and
the other sprouts thorns. Similarly, for
all thirteen years, both [Yaakov and Eisav]
went back and forth to the beis hasefer.
After thirteen years one would go to the
batei midrashos and the other would go
to the houses of avodah zarah."
(Bereishis Rabbah, Parashas Toldos 63:10)

INTRODUCTION TO STAGE IV

Avraham and his descendants were chosen from among all the nations and were given the land of Eretz Yisrael, as Hashem said to Avraham, "To your descendants I gave this land."[232]

However, not all his children were included in this promise; only Yitzchak was considered the descendant of Avraham, not Yishmael, nor any of the other children of Avraham. When Hashem said to Avraham, "Because in Yitzchak your descendants will be called,"[233] this excluded Yishmael and the other children of Hagar. And just as Avraham was chosen from among all the nations of the world to be the first forefather of Yisrael, Yitzchak was chosen from among the children of Avraham to be the second forefather of Yisrael.

Yitzchak was selected to be his father's successor because he was found to be worthy of carrying on Avraham's spiritual legacy. Yitzchak not only followed in Avraham's footsteps, but he built upon and added to the edifice of spiritual greatness that his father Avraham had established.[234]

The selection process continued with the children of Yitzchak. Yaakov was chosen over Eisav to carry on Yitzchak's legacy. Hashem said to Avraham, "Because **in** Yitzchak your descendants will be called." This verse implies that not all the children of Yitzchak were considered

---

232 *Parashas Lech Lecha* 15:18.
233 *Parashas Vayeira* 21:12.
234 *Teshuvos Chasam Sofer, Orach Chaim* §208; *Michtav Mi'Eliyahu, chelek* II, p. 205.

descendants of Avraham; only Yaakov, but not Eisav, would inherit Avraham's legacy.[235]

However, the selection of Yaakov over Eisav was not predetermined, nor inevitable, unlike the selection of Yitzchak over Avraham's other children:

- Avraham's "other" children were born from a concubine, and were not on equal status with Yitzchak.
- In contrast, Eisav was born equal to Yaakov; they shared the same mother and even the same womb. In fact, Eisav, as the firstborn, had a higher rank than Yaakov.

It was ultimately Eisav's deeds, and not his lineage, that prevented him from taking his rightful place among the forefathers of Yisrael.

---

235   *Rashi, Parashas Vayeitzei* 28:15.

FOURTEEN

THE PARTING OF TWINS

The Torah describes Eisav as a hunter who spent his time in the fields, and Yaakov as one who sat in the tent learning Torah.[236] *Rashi* relates that when Yaakov and Eisav reached the age of thirteen years old, Yaakov dedicated himself to studying Torah, while Eisav dedicated his time to outdoor pursuits.[237] Yet this did not deter their father Yitzchak from attempting to crown Eisav with his blessings.

Why was it not apparent to Yitzchak that Yaakov was more suited to be his spiritual heir than Eisav?

Yitzchak believed that Eisav's material pursuits did not detract from his potential to become a forefather of Yisrael. The *Chasam Sofer*[238] explains that, ideally, the relationship between Yaakov and Eisav would have resembled that of Yissachar and Zevulun. The tribes of Yissachar and Zevulun established a partnership in which the tribe of Zevulun engaged in commerce and provided for the tribe of Yissachar, who was occupied with learning Torah.[239] It could have been the same for Eisav and Yaakov; Eisav would have spent his time out in the field to provide support for Yaakov's Torah learning. In this way, Eisav's predilection for the field did not contradict his ideal role as a supporter of Torah. Eisav

---

236 *Parashas Toldos* 25:26.
237 Ibid.
238 *Sefer Toras Moshe, Parashas Toldos*; see also *Malbim, Parashas Toldos* 27:1.
239 *Rashi, Parashas V'zos HaBerachah* 33:18, *Parashas Vayechi* 49:13.

was not fit for the rigor of constant Torah study, but he was well-suited to fill the role as a provider for Torah. If he had chosen to follow the path of serving Hashem, he would have provided for all of Yaakov's needs and allowed him to learn without any distractions.

Although the primary purpose of the world is the study of Torah, Zevulun's role as its supporter is no less essential than Yissachar's role, because his support makes Yissachar's Torah learning possible, as the Mishnah states, "If there is no flour there is no Torah."[240] According to the *Chasam Sofer*,[241] the supporters of Torah are rewarded even more than those who learn Torah. This is because Hashem rewards us for our deeds in accordance with the degree of difficulty. One who supports Torah does not experience the sweetness of Torah that Torah scholars enjoy. Consequently, his act of supporting Torah scholars is pure without any taint of self-interest and therefore, his reward is greater.

In this ideal environment of true spiritual partnership, both Eisav and Yaakov would have had a place within the hierarchy of Yisrael. Yaakov and Eisav would have both been chosen as forefathers of Yisrael. The twelve Holy Tribes of Yisrael would have been born from between Eisav and Yaakov. Eisav would have married Leah, the firstborn of Lavan, while Yaakov would have only married Lavan's younger daughter Rachel. Eisav, as the firstborn, would have been given a double portion in the twelve tribes — eight of the twelve would have been born to him. Yaakov would have been given a single portion of four sons out of the twelve holy tribes.

Leah was aware that Eisav would not fill his role as a forefather of Yisrael and she cried to Hashem that she not be forced to marry him.[242] Her prayers were answered and she married Yaakov instead. Nevertheless, eight out of the twelve tribes were born from Leah and her concubine. As Eisav's intended wife, Leah was destined to give birth to a double portion of the tribes and she did lose this right, despite her marriage to Yaakov instead of Eisav.

---

240   *Pirkei Avos* 3:17.
241   *Sefer Toras Moshe, Parashas Toldos.*
242   *Midrash Rabbah, Parashas Vayeitzei* 71:2.

In light of Eisav's intended role, we can understand Yitzchak's desire to bless Eisav. Yitzchak was fully aware that while Yaakov sat in the tents of Shem and Eiver learning Torah, Eisav spent his time in the fields.[243] Nevertheless, Yitzchak wanted to bless Eisav that Hashem should provide him with the means to support Torah. Yitzchak tailored the blessings to suit Eisav's role as a supporter of Torah, and wanted to gift him with fertile, bountiful land and an abundance of grain and wine.

The blessing intended for Eisav would not have excluded Yaakov from the fulfillment of his role as a forefather of Yisrael. To the contrary, the blessing that Eisav was to receive would have helped Yaakov fill his role as a Torah scholar. Both Yaakov and Eisav were to receive blessings from Yitzchak that would enable them to fulfill their destinies. Yaakov was to be blessed with the spiritual legacy of Avraham, which was eminently suited to him with his single-minded devotion to spiritual matters. The material blessings that Eisav was to receive were appropriate for him, as he was to utilize these blessings as a means to support his brother, enabling Yaakov to grow in Torah without the distraction of finding his own means of support.[244]

However, this arrangement between Yaakov and Eisav was not to be. Although Yaakov honored his part of the deal, Eisav was not compliant. Why did Eisav reject his part within the hierarchy of Yisrael? It is not that Eisav was not interested in having a role in the Jewish People, Yisrael. To the contrary, Eisav valued Yitzchak's blessings and understood their spiritual power, which is apparent from his great and bitter cry upon finding out that Yaakov received the blessings intended for him.[245]

Despite this, Eisav was not willing to make the sacrifices necessary to fulfill his intended role as forefather of the Jewish People. Eisav was not eager to share his wealth with Yaakov, which his role as a supporter of Torah would have required him to do. He was also unwilling to live a life

---

243   *Parashas Toldos* 25:26.
244   *Chasam Sofer, Sefer Toras Moshe, Parashas Toldos; Malbim, Parashas Toldos* 27:1.
245   *Parashas Toldos* 27:34.

of self-sacrifice and sanctity, which is essential for a forefather of Yisrael. The essence of sanctity is to abstain from excessive physical pleasures in this world. Unlike Yaakov, who wanted nothing more than "bread to eat and a garment to wear,"[246] Eisav could never be satisfied with that. This can be seen in the very telling exchange between Yaakov and Eisav when they meet upon Yaakov's return from the house of Lavan. Eisav boasts, "I have much,"[247] meaning he had excessive possessions, much more than he needed."[248] Yaakov, on the other hand, says, "I have everything,"[249] meaning he had just what he needed.[250] Eisav's insatiable appetite for material goods made it impossible for him to achieve sanctity in this world and to become a forefather of the future nation of Yisrael. With his path blocked from achieving sanctity, Eisav decided instead to further entrench his standing in this world, and traded his share in the next world for Yaakov's share in this world. [251]

Having sold his share in this world, Yaakov lived an especially tortured existence; he was pursued by Eisav and Lavan, both of whom wanted to destroy him. When he finally escaped their clutches and he felt he could finally live in peace, Hashem told him that it is sufficient for the righteous to have a place in the next world; they cannot expect to live in peace in this world as well.[252] Yaakov then experienced the anguish of the sale of Yosef by his brothers and his belief that Yosef had been killed. He lived through another twenty-two torturous years before he was finally reunited with Yosef in Egypt.

Yaakov accepted his tortured existence in this world out of an appreciation for the spiritual paradise of the next world. Eisav, however, was not completely at peace with his choice to give up his share in the next world for a larger share in this world, since he understood the spiritual benefits of the next world. When Eisav confronted Yaakov

---

246 *Parashas Vayeitzei* 28:20.
247 *Parashas Vayishlach* 33:9.
248 *Rashi, Parashas Vayishlach* 33:11.
249 *Parashas Vayishlach* 33:11.
250 *Rashi, Parashas Vayishlach* 33:11.
251 *Tanna D'Bei Eliyahu, perek* 19.
252 *Rashi, Parashas Vayeishev* 37:1.

on the latter's return from the house of Lavan and witnessed his large family and many possessions, he began to regret the trade he had made. It occurred to him that Yaakov's extra share in the next world would not be at the expense of material success in this world. He requested a reversal of the trade and that they share both this world and the next.

However, in this Eisav was mistaken: one who indulges himself in this world will find himself shortchanged in the next world. Indeed, Yaakov did not partake in the pleasures of this world at all. He continued to live a life of austerity despite his wealth, in the spirit of his wealthy descendant Rebbi, who swore at the time of his death that he had not had any pleasure from his riches at all.[253] Yaakov partook from this world only what he needed for serving Hashem.[254]

In light of this, we can understand the midrash that states that Eisav rejected the *bris milah*.[255] The mitzvah of *bris milah* helps us curb our physical desires and achieve a measure of sanctity in this world. Eisav did not have the will to curb his physical desires at all. Eisav did understand the importance of sanctity and wished to achieve it, however, he was in no hurry to do so; he believed he would achieve sanctity toward the end of his life and there was no point depriving himself in his younger years. Much like Bilaam who prayed to die the death of *yesharim* (our holy forefathers who are called *yesharim*) while

---

253   *Maseches Kesuvos* 104a.

254   *Maharal Sefer Netzach Yisrael, perek* 19. The Talmud (*Maseches Berachos* 5b) states that when Rabbi Elazar was ill, his students paid him a visit and found that he was crying. They asked, "Why are you crying? If it is because you did not merit wealth in this world, one does not merit to have two tables, i.e., wealth in this world along with a full portion in the next world." *Tosafos* amends the text to: "Not everyone can achieve two tables," because while it is possible to achieve both, such as Rebbi who enjoyed wealth in this world, not everyone merits this. The *Maharal* insists that the original text is correct because, in truth, it is not possible to merit two tables; one who partakes in the pleasures in this world will inevitably find his portion in the next world diminished. Rebbi may have been blessed with great wealth, but he did not benefit from it at all. He used his wealth only for the bare minimum that he needed for his service of Hashem. In the end, we need to choose: which world do we want?

255   *Pirkei D'Rabbi Eliezer, perek* 29.

living a life of sin,[256] Eisav wished to die as a holy person while living a life of depravity.

Chazal tell us that until he was forty years old, Eisav entrapped married women into his lair. When he turned forty, he said, "My father, Yitzchak, married at forty years old, I too will marry at forty years old."[257] Of course, they were worlds apart:

- Yitzchak only married at forty because until that age he occupied himself in the pursuit of sanctity, so much so that Chazal refer to Yitzchak as an *olah temimah* [258] — an unblemished *korban olah* (burnt offering).

- Eisav wanted to follow in the path of his father and achieve sanctity by marrying at forty, but marrying at forty was only commendable for one who had occupied himself in sanctity until that age. For Eisav who had lived a life of sin until then, marrying at forty would not help him achieve sanctity.

Sanctity can only be achieved in incremental steps, not in one big leap. One who spends a lifetime in the pursuit of physical indulgence will find it impossible to reverse course at the end of his life, despite his best efforts.[259]

The *Malbim* explains that unlike Yitzchak, Rivkah intuited that Eisav refused to accept this role as supporter of Yaakov's Torah learning. Without this support, it was imperative that Yaakov be given the means to support himself independently. Furthermore, Rivkah foresaw that the material blessings that were to be given to Eisav would conversely end up being used in a manner that would be detrimental to Yaakov and inhibit his spiritual growth. Eisav would ultimately use the bounty he received as a means to oppress and persecute Yaakov, making it even more difficult for him to learn Torah. Therefore, Rivkah took matters into her own hands and arranged for Yaakov to receive the blessings

---

256 *Ksav Sofer, Parashas Balak.*
257 *Rashi, Parashas Toldos 26:34.*
258 *Rashi, Parashas Toldos 26:2.*
259 *Reishis Chochmah, Shaar HaTeshuvah, perek 5.*

intended for Eisav. As a result of Rivkah's intervention, Yaakov received the material blessings of Yitzchak, which gave him the ability to achieve earthly material success and support himself independently.[260] Later on, he would receive the spiritual blessings of Avraham as well, which would enable him to succeed in his Torah pursuits.[261]

---

260   *Malbim, Parashas Toldos* 27:5.
261   *Parashas Vayeitzei* 28:4.

FOR THE JEWISH People to thrive, it is important for those who are not fit for the rigors of Torah study to take the role of supporters of Torah. Ideally, Eisav could have filled this role, but he failed to do so. Instead, both roles would have to be filled by the descendants of Yaakov, with some of his descendants learning Torah, such as the tribe of Yissachar, and others, such as the Tribe of Zevulun, supporting the Torah scholars.

FIFTEEN

A YISRAEL MUMAR

A fter losing the blessings to Yaakov, Eisav continued in the same path and distanced himself even further from the ways of his great forefathers. In his contempt for anything holy, he divested himself one by one of the spiritual assets he had inherited:

- He had previously forfeited his rights as a firstborn in the spiritual inheritance of his father Yitzchak in exchange for a porion of lentil soup, but had still retained a single portion.

- Eisav forfeited all rights to the spiritual inheritance of his father Yitzchak upon Yaakov's return from Charan. Eisav accepted Yaakov's gifts with the acknowledgment that Yaakov had sole rights to Yitzchak's blessings.[262] However, Eisav retained his rights to a portion in Eretz Yisrael.

- Eisav forfeited his rights to Eretz Yisrael with his refusal to pay the entry price — to be a sojourner in a foreign land for four hundred years. He abandoned Eretz Yisrael and took up residence in Mount Seir instead.[263]

- Finally, Eisav sold Yaakov his rights to burial in the Cave of Machpeilah in exchange for the money that Yaakov earned in Lavan's house.[264]

---

262 *Rashi, Parashas Vayishlach* 33:9.
263 *Rashi, Parashas Vayishlach* 36:7.
264 *Rashi, Parashas Vayechi* 50:5.

A common theme in all of Eisav's spiritual divestment was his willingness to exchange spiritual legacies for material benefits. The spiritual legacies had value to Eisav — he would not have given them away for nothing — but material benefits were more valuable to him.

Yet, despite Eisav's best efforts to distance himself from Yitzchak's legacy in every way, and his unworthiness of being a forefather of Yisrael, he was not completely cut off from his legacy as a son of Yitzchak and grandson of Avraham. The Torah calls Eisav a *yisrael mumar* — a wayward Jew.[265] Since it was his deeds, and not his lineage, that prevented Eisav from becoming a member of Yisrael in good standing, he did not lose his inheritance completely, and he received diluted versions of the true legacy. The land of Mount Seir, where Eisav took residence, was included among the ten nations that was promised to Avraham, and will become part of Eretz Yisrael in the times of Mashiach.[266] And although Yaakov and Leah would be the fourth and last couple buried in the Cave of Machpeilah, Eisav's head was buried there.[267]

Since Eisav retained a portion in Yisrael even after he was rejected, the potential still existed for his progeny to fulfill his intended role — supporting Torah learning. The *Chasam Sofer* maintains that the model of this ideal was the relationship between Antoninus Caesar and Rebbi. This collaboration was so significant that it was foretold while Yaakov and Eisav were still in the womb.[268] When Rivkah was pregnant with twins, it was revealed to her that there were two [future] nations in her womb,[269] and *Rashi* explains that the two nations are a reference to Rebbi (Rabbi Yehudah HaNasi) and Antoninus Caesar.[270] Antoninus, in his position as the Roman Caesar, developed a deep admiration for Rebbi and resolved to assist the Torah sages by dismissing them from

---

265 *Kiddushin* 18a.
266 *Rashi, Parashas Devarim* 2:5.
267 *Maseches Sotah* 13a.
268 *Chasam Sofer, Sefer Toras Moshe* 25:23.
269 *Parashas Toldos* 25:23.
270 Ibid.

their tax obligations.[271] During his reign, the Jewish People enjoyed a rare respite from Roman persecution and a period of peace and tranquility was ushered in. This gave the sages the opportunity to gather together all of the Torah students in Eretz Yisrael for the purpose of clarifying the Oral Torah.[272] Thus, as a result of this rare cooperation between the progeny of Yaakov and Eisav, Rebbi and his students managed to compile the six orders of the Mishnah, a massive undertaking that would not have otherwise been possible.[273] Unfortunately, however, this type of cooperation between Yisrael and Eisav was all too rare, more the exception than the rule. For the most part, the progeny of Eisav have followed the lead of their forefather Eisav who relinquished his role as a supporter of Torah. Instead of supporting Yisrael's Torah learning, they have done everything in their power to hinder it.

Having once been considered part of Yisrael, and with a continuous potential for a partnership, Eisav and his descendants never received the status of a separate nation, and they are not counted among the seventy nations.[274] As a result of their lack of identity as a distinct nation, they are called an *am bazui* — an inferior nation. They have neither their own language nor manner of writing, and they were forced to adopt it from other nations.[275]

Since Eisav's descendants did not become a distinct nation, they lack a conduit for blessing. All other nations are under their own *mazal*, which shapes the identity of the nation and acts a conduit to bring the nations heavenly blessing.[276] The Jewish People are an exception as they are directly under the Divine Providence. Eisav was meant to be part of the Jewish People and to bask directly under the Divine Providence; as such, his descendants were not placed under a specific *mazal* like the other non-Jewish nations. However, when he relinquished his rights to the Jewish People he was removed from the direct Divine Providence. Thus,

---

271   *Maseches Avodah Zarah* 10a.
272   *Rashi, Bava Metzia* 33b.
273   *Legacy of Sinai*, based on *Igeres Rav Sherira Gaon* 1:2.
274   *Maharal, Derush Al HaTorah.*
275   *Maseches Avodah Zarah* 10a, and *Rashi.*
276   Rabbeinu Bachya, *Parashas Toldos* 25:28.

Eisav and his descendants were left without any direct or indirect conduit with which to receive blessing in this world.

In light of the above, we can readily understand Eisav's bitter cry upon his realization that Yaakov had received his blessings. Yitzchak's blessings were to be his lifeline, the only means by which he would receive bounty directly from Heaven without the need for a *mazal*. When the blessings were given to Yaakov instead, he was left without any means for Divine blessing, not by the *mazalos* and not directly from Hashem. Therefore, even after Yitzchak insisted that he had given all of the blessings to Yaakov and that he had nothing to bless him with, Eisav begged him for at least one blessing that would give him a path to success. [277]

Yitzchak acquiesced to Eisav's supplication and he blessed him, "You shall live by your sword."[278] Although not a tangible blessing in the classical sense, for Eisav, Yitzchak's assurance that he would live by his sword was a blessing. As a result of this "blessing," Eisav received his heavenly bounty through the *mazal* of *ma'adim*, the *mazal* of destruction.[279] Unlike the *mazalos* of the seventy nations, Eisav's *mazal* was not a conduit for blessing, but it bestowed on Eisav the capacity to rampage and destroy.[280] Lacking any concrete source of blessing, Eisav had no choice but to pillage the blessings of other nations by the blade of his sword. Thus, for Eisav, living by the sword was his only path to success.

Although Yaakov took the blessings away from Eisav, nevertheless Eisav ultimately received a path to Yitzchak's blessing. Yitzchak blessed Eisav, "And when you are aggrieved you shall take off his yoke from your neck,"[281] meaning that when Yaakov or his descendants fail to follow in the path of the Torah, Eisav can take the blessings away from them. This is because Yaakov and his descendants received Yitzchak's blessings conditionally — only when they engage in the will of Hashem,

---

277   *Parashas Toldos* 27:38.

278   *Parashas Toldos* 27:40.

279   *Beraisa D'Shmuel, perek* 9, *Ramban, Parashas Acharei Mos* 16:8, *Chasam Sofer, Sefer Toras Moshe, Parashas Pinchas.*

280   Rabbeinu Bachya, *Parashas Lech Lecha* 12:3.

281   Ibid.

but not when they abandon Hashem and the Torah.[282] When the Jewish nation defies Hashem's will, the Divine blessing is diverted from the descendants of Yaakov and given to Eisav, as the Talmud relates: "The coffers of Eisav are filled from the ruins of Yisrael."[283]

Thus, despite Eisav's tenuous status as an outsider to the seventy nations, he still had a path to success: the downfall of the Jewish people. This potential was realized when the descendants of Eisav founded the Roman empire. The *Maharsha*[284] explains that the Roman empire had its source in the destruction of the First Holy Temple, whereupon the benefits that had been channeled from Hashem to the Jewish people in the merit of the *avodah* in the Holy Temple were diverted to Eisav's descendants.

This explains how Eisav's descendants received great power and influence but it does not explain how they received the lands of their rule — Rome and Central Europe — after taking leave of Har Se'ir, their original place of residence. The lands of the world had been divided into seventy parts and had been parceled out to the seventy nations, which did not include Eisav's descendants.

Rashi explains that Eisav was given the land of Italya shel Yavan as part of Yitzchak's blessings.[285]

How did Yitzchak have the power to give Eisav a land, considering he had just finished telling him he had nothing left to give him?[286] The answer is that Yitzchak gave Eisav a land that did not yet exist and thus had not been given away to anyone else. The Talmud reveals that the existence of Italya shel Yavan came about as a result of the sin of Shlomo HaMelech. When Shlomo and the Jewish people sinned with idolatry, the angel Gavriel inserted a reed into the ocean, and that reed eventually collected enough dirt to become inhabitable, until it ultimately

---

282   Rabbeinu Bachya, *Parashas Toldos* 27:39.
283   *Maseches Megillah* 6a.
284   *Chiddushei Aggados, Maseches Sanhedrin* 21b.
285   *Parashas Toldos* 27:39.
286   Ibid., verse 37.

became Italya shel Yavan.[287] The *Maharsha*[288] explains that when Shlomo HaMelech and the Jewish People sinned, the seeds were sown for the eventual destruction of the Holy Temple and the subsequent rise of the descendants of Eisav in the form of the Roman Empire. Thus, it was also at this time that Hashem began the process of creating a land that would eventually become the homeland of the descendants of Eisav.

Since Eisav's fortune depends on Yisrael throwing off the yoke of the mitzvos, he and his descendants have a special interest in preventing Yisrael from keeping the Torah. In particular, the nation of Amalek, who descends from Eisav, has always been a thorn at the side of Yisrael, doing its utmost to prevent Yisrael from fulfilling Hashem's will.

What is Eisav's strategy for preventing the Jewish nation from adhering to the will of Hashem, and thus empowering itself? They accomplish this by the blade of their sword, persecuting the descendants of Yaakov and denying them their basic needs. This forces the Jewish People to abandon the study halls of Torah in pursuit of their livelihood. In a reversal of their intended role as supporters of Torah, Eisav and his descendants accomplish more for themselves as persecutors of Torah. Consistent with this, the Talmud relates that when Onkelos (known for the *Targum Onkelos*) contemplated converting to Judaism, he was advised by Titus (a descendant of Eisav and the former commander of the Roman army that destroyed the Beis Hamikdash) to oppress the Jewish People rather than joining them because "whoever oppresses the Jewish People achieves greatness." [289]

---

287   *Maseches Sanhedrin* 21b.
288   *Chidushei Aggados*, ibid.
289   *Maseches Gittin* 55b.

DESPITE HIS BEST efforts, Eisav could not rid himself completely of all vestige of his spiritual inheritance. Eisav and his descendants could claim their spiritual legacy at any time and fulfill the role of supporters of Torah. Even when they refuse to do so (the vast majority of the time) they take the blessing from the descendants of Yaakov when the Jewish People defy the will of Hashem.

SIXTEEN

GID HANASHEH – YAAKOV'S VULNERABILITY

Yitzchak had given to Yaakov the material blessings that were meant for Eisav, which blessed his endeavors with material success and made it possible for Yaakov to support himself independently. The blessings, however, did not automatically shower Yaakov with means of support. Yaakov would have to disrupt his learning and go out and earn his livelihood. This was less than ideal because Yaakov's place was in the study halls of Torah, not in the fields. As a consequence of Eisav refusing his mission and forcing Yaakov to pick up the slack, Yaakov and his descendants would no longer be able to dedicate themselves solely to the pursuit of learning Torah.

The lack of material support would hamper the Jewish People's growth in Torah and make them spiritually vulnerable. The negative impact from a dearth of material good manifests itself in two ways:

- It robs Torah scholars of the time they would otherwise use in pursuit of Torah scholarship.
- The pursuit of a livelihood can result in the excessive pursuit of materialism.

This new reality had an immediate impact. After Yaakov received Yitzchak's blessings and fortified himself with Torah learning in the study halls of Shem and Eiver,[290] Yaakov traveled to Charan for the purpose of marrying one of Lavan's daughters, as instructed by his father. On his way to Charan, Yaakov was accosted by Eisav's son Elifaz, who robbed him of all possessions.[291] Thus, he arrived at Lavan's house penniless, making it necessary for him to work for Lavan for twenty years. Thus, Rivkah's premonition about Eisav's unsuitability to receive Yitzchak's blessing was already apparent. Eisav not only refused to support Yaakov, but also sent his son to deprive Yaakov of any material items he did possess.

Yaakov's deprivation forced him to toil day and night in the house of Lavan. This took both a physical and spiritual toll on Yaakov. The lack of support from Eisav not only took Yaakov away from the study halls of Torah, but also resulted in an excessive pursuit of materialism, at least by the exacting standards of a righteous person like Yaakov.

The *Kli Yakar* maintains that Yaakov's indifference to material pursuits was put to the test by the angel of Eisav.[292] When Yaakov returned from Lavan's house, he crossed the Yaabok River to retrieve small earthenware jars. Due to his deprivation, Yaakov's hard-earned possessions were especially dear.[293] However, by risking his life to retrieve these jars, Yaakov put more value on his possessions than was necessary[294] and this gave the angel of Eisav the opportunity to instigate a confrontation with him.[295] Although Yaakov ultimately overcame him, the angel managed to harm Yaakov in the area where

---

290 *Rashi, Parashas Toldos* 48:9.

291 *Rashi, Parashas Vayeitzei* 29:11.

292 *Parashas Vayishlach* 32:25.

293 Chazal declare that a person prefers one *kav* (a measure) of his own produce [that he worked hard for], rather than nine *kavim* belonging to his friend (*Maseches Bava Metzia* 38a, and *Rashi*). Although the principle that the righteous are very scrupulous with their money applies to all righteous people, the fact that Chazal derive this lesson specifically from Yaakov, and particularly from the story of his encounter with Eisav and his angel, could be understood to emphasize that this trait was of particular significance to Yaakov.

294 *Parashas Vayishlach* 32:25 and *Rashi*.

295 The Talmud explains that righteous people are very scrupulous with their money, and even small utensils are valuable to them (*Maseches Chullin* 9a). Nevertheless, according to the *Kli Yakar*, Yaakov should not have risked his life to retrieve them.

he was vulnerable — the upper thigh — which caused a dislocation of the *gid hanasheh* tendon.

Why was Yaakov most vulnerable in the thigh area? The *Chafetz Chaim* explains in the name of the *Zohar* that the *gid hanasheh* symbolizes the supporters of Torah. The thigh gives support to the body and it allows a person to stand upright, in the same way that Torah supporters hold up the Torah scholars with material support, allowing them to pursue Torah scholarship with peace of mind. Without the supporters of Torah, the Torah scholars are metaphorically crippled in their pursuit of Torah scholarship.[296] The thigh symbolized the support of Torah scholars, and since Yaakov showed weakness in this area when he risked his life to retrieve small jars, the angel of Eisav was empowered to dislocate a tendon in Yaakov thigh and cripple him.

Although Yaakov was crippled by the dislocation, this disability was short-lived. Yaakov dedicated himself anew to an ascetic lifestyle and his ever-so-slight inclination for material goods became a thing of the past. The next morning, the sun rose early for him and healed him sufficiently to allow him to walk, albeit with a limp.[297] Even the limp was only temporary,[298] as the Torah states that "Yaakov arrived whole in the city of Shechem;"[299] meaning that upon his arrival in Shechem he was no longer limping. Yaakov survived the encounter with Eisav, both with the angel of Eisav and subsequently with Eisav himself, completely intact; whole in body, property, and Torah.[300]

Thus, we see that Yaakov managed to overcome this vulnerability of a lack of material support.[301] This symbolized that future generations of Torah scholars would manage to overcome a lack of material support from their brethren. Although it is more challenging, Torah scholars

---

296   *Sefer Chomas HaDaas, Chasimas HaSefer, Maamar Sheni*, in the *Hagahah*.

297   *Rashi, Parashas Vayishlach 32:32.*

298   *Sefer Akeidas Yitzchak, Parashas Vayishlach.*

299   *Parashas Vayishlach 33:18.*

300   *Rashi*, ibid.

301   Although *Rashi* in Chumash comments that his Torah learning remained intact despite his years in the house of Lavan, *Rashi* in the Talmud (*Maseches Shabbos* 33b) says that his Torah learning remained intact despite the travails of his travels.

can succeed in their Torah learning even with insufficient support, just as Yaakov overcame the lack of support from Eisav.

How can Yaakov's descendants overcome the deprivation forced upon them by the descendants of Eisav? They can accomplish this by following in the footsteps of their forefather Yaakov who made do with the bare minimum. By adopting the characteristic of *histapkus b'muat* — eschewing excessive materialism — the Jewish People are assured that they will have the peace of mind to pursue spiritual pursuits. This is because, regardless of the degree of Eisav's persecution, the Jewish People will always have the minimum of material goods needed for their survival, as we recite in the *Birkas Hamazon* (after-blessing on bread),"I was young and also I grew old and I have not seen a righteous person abandoned and his children seeking bread."[302] A minimum of materialism should be sufficient for Torah scholars, as the Mishnah states, "This is the way of the Torah: You shall eat your bread with salt, and you shall drink your water in measure and you shall sleep on the ground and live a life of affliction."[303]

A critical ingredient for *histapkus b'muat* is *bitachon* — the belief that Hashem is always with us and does only good for us. One who has *bitachon* will never worry about his livelihood, because he knows that Hashem provides a source of livelihood for all living beings from the smallest to the largest. Chazal tell us that when the prophet Yirmiyah exhorted the Jewish people to learn Torah, they responded, "How can we take off from our work to learn Torah, how will we earn our livelihood?" Yirmiyah took out the cylinder with the manna that was stored next to the Aron and displayed it to them. He said, "This was the provisions of your ancestors; Hashem has many emissaries to provide for those that fear Him."[304]

Since Torah scholars are capable of succeeding, despite a lack of support, the obligation to support Torah scholars is not primarily for the good of the Torah scholars, but rather for the good of the Torah supporters. The supporters of Torah gain a share in the Torah learning

---

302   *Sefer Tehillim* 37:25.
303   *Pirkei Avos* 6:4.
304   *Mechilta, Parashas Beshalach*, brought in *Rashi, Shemos* 16:32.

of the Torah scholars, and will also be blessed with Divine help in their business endeavors.[305] Moreover, the primary manner for a Jewish person to achieve closeness with Hashem is through the Torah scholars. The *Rambam* explains[306] that the Torah commandment "To Him you shall cleave"[307] cannot be done directly because Hashem is a consuming fire, and the only way to fulfill this mitzvah is to cleave to the sages and to their students.[308] By providing the sages with their needs and enabling them to learn Torah, we are by extension cleaving to Hashem.

Although Yaakov's limp was ultimately healed, the Torah states: "Therefore B'nei Yisrael do not eat the *gid hanasheh* to this day."[309] This prohibition symbolizes Yaakov's encounter with Eisav and his subsequent recovery. By abstaining from eating the *gid hanasheh*, B'nei Yisrael are reminded not just of the imperative of supporting Torah scholars, but also that the privilege of doing so is primarily for their own benefit.[310]

---

305   Rav Zalman Sorotzkin, *Sefer HaDeah V'Hadibur*, chap. 1.
306   *Hilchos Deyos* 6:2.
307   *Parashas Eikev* 11:22.
308   *Sifri*, ibid.
309   *Parashas Vayishlach* 32:33.
310   Rav Zalman Sorotzkin, *Sefer HaDeah V'Hadibur*, chap. 1.

EISAV'S FAILURE TO fill his intended role of supporting Torah scholars left Yaakov vulnerable. However, Yaakov, like all Torah scholars, made do with the basic minimum and thus overcame the lack of support.

AFTERWORD

Yaakov and Eisav both had the potential to be forefathers of Yisrael; Yaakov as a Torah scholar and Eisav as a supporter of Torah. Yaakov fulfilled his potential and earned the right to be a forefather of Yisrael, while Eisav failed to do so and willingly sold out his rights to this role. Eisav's lust for the physical pleasures of this world overcame his intellect and allowed him to be convinced that he could enjoy the pleasures of this world without compromising his share in the next world. He reasoned that after spending his life enjoying the fruits of this world he would work on achieving sanctity toward the end of his life. He did not take into account that sanctity is a gradual process that cannot be achieved in one leap.

Yitzchak saw only the good in Eisav — his sincere desire for spiritual achievement — and did not recognize that Eisav was in no hurry to achieve spirituality, and was in the meantime living a life of depravity. His mother, Rivkah, realized this and she arranged for Yaakov to receive the blessings that were intended for Eisav. Eisav's failure meant that Yaakov and his descendants would have to fill the role intended for Eisav and his descendants — the support of Torah scholars. This would force Yaakov and his descendants out of the study halls of Torah and leave them spiritually vulnerable. Eisav and his descendants would take full advantage and persecute the Jewish People in an effort to deprive them of their ability to support themselves

Despite Eisav's noncompliance with his intended role, he retained his birthright as a descendant of Yitzchak and Yaakov. Eisav's descendants could choose to fill their intended role as supporters of Torah and would reap the spiritual benefits. Antoninus was one descendant who filled this role, and he enabled Rabbi Yehudah HaNasi to establish the six orders of the Mishnah. Even when the descendants of Eisav reject their role as supporters of Torah, they have a path to the blessings of Yitzchak when the Jewish People abandon the way of Torah. Eisav's descendants over the years have persecuted the Jewish People in an effort to strip them of their blessings and take them for themselves.

However, despite Eisav and his descendants' best efforts, they will never be fully successful in their persecution of Yisrael. The Jewish People were given the guarantee that "[the Torah] will not be forgotten from among their descendants."[311] The Torah has always been a life raft for the Jewish People, keeping them afloat among the vicious waves and stormy waters of the non-Jewish nations. When Yaakov and his descendants were exiled to Egypt and were eventually subjugated and enslaved, the Torah of their forefathers would stand for them and allow them to survive as a distinct people. Yaakov foresaw this, and therefore, before he set foot in Egypt, he sent his son Yehudah ahead of him to establish a study hall of Torah there, which provided a spiritual haven in the midst of the depraved environment of Egypt. This helped his descendants hold onto their spiritual legacy throughout their lengthy exile in Egypt and eventually emerge as a nation of six hundred thousand, who would fifty days later receive the Torah.

---

311 *Parashas Vayeilech* 31:21.

FROM BONDAGE TO FREEDOM: EXODUS FROM EGYPT

"AND ALSO I WILL HEAR THE CRIES OF B'NEI YISRAEL" – BECAUSE THEY DID NOT DOUBT ME. AND ALSO, EVEN THOUGH B'NEI YISRAEL IN THAT GENERATION WERE NOT ACTING PROPERLY, I HEARD THEIR CRIES AS A RESULT OF THE COVENANT THAT I ESTABLISHED WITH THEIR FOREFATHERS.

(BEREISHIS RABBAH 6:4)

INTRODUCTION TO STAGE V

After Avraham successfully waged war with the four kings, Hashem promised to give him and his descendants Eretz Yisrael. Avraham questioned this promise, and asked, "How will I know that I will inherit it?"[312]

How is it that Avraham, the paragon of faith, questioned the promise of Hashem?

Avraham was not questioning whether the promise of Hashem would be fulfilled; he never harbored any doubt that Hashem would keep His promise. Rather, he was expressing his concern that his descendants would one day stray from the path of the Torah and be forced to relinquish Eretz Yisrael.[313] Avraham knew that the Canaanim, who occupied Eretz Yisrael at the time, would ultimately be forced to forfeit the land as a result of their sins, and he was afraid that the same would happen to his descendants. Hashem had promised the land to his descendants, but the promise from Hashem was not guaranteed; it was conditional on the continued righteousness of the recipients and could be altered or revoked, as warranted.[314] Thus, Avraham's reasoning had some merit and was not a symptom of lack of faith.

Nevertheless, after the Akeidah, Hashem did, in fact, guarantee His promise to give Eretz Yisrael to the descendants of Avraham, alleviating his concern that the land would one day be taken away from his

---

312 *Parashas Lech Lecha* 15:8.
313 *Rashi, Parashas Lech Lecha* 15:6.
314 *Maharal, Sefer Gur Aryeh, Parashas Lech Lecha* 15:6.

descendants.[315] Why did Hashem guarantee His promise to Avraham if the continued righteousness of his descendants was uncertain?

The answer is enlightening. While it was indeed possible that Avraham's descendants would stray from the path of righteousness, it was impossible that they would ever lose their faith in Hashem. This is because faith in Hashem was such an integral part of Avraham's being that it became a hereditary trait that would be passed on to his descendants. The Jewish People are called *ma'aminim b'nei ma'aminim* — believers, the sons of believers,[316] since their faith derives from their forefathers, the original *ma'aminim*. Thus, there would never be a reason for Hashem to revoke His promise and displace Avraham's descendants from their status as the Chosen Nation. Although the Jewish nation did eventually sin and were exiled from Eretz Yisrael, their faith in Hashem never wavered, which was assurance that they would eventually repent and be returned to the Land.[317]

Furthermore, B'nei Yisrael are not only *b'nei ma'aminim* (children of believers), they are also *ma'aminim* (believers) in their own right. The *Chasam Sofer* maintains that in addition to their inherited faith, Avraham's descendants also achieved faith in Hashem through their own efforts. Eretz Yisrael would be given to Avraham's children in the merit of the faith that they would acquire independently of the faith they inherited from their forefathers.[318] In order to bring forth this latent faith, Hashem decreed that the Jewish nation would be exiled to Egypt. The challenges that the Jewish nation would face in Egypt would serve as the means to propel them to an elevated level of faith through their own actions.

Thus, when Avraham asked, "How will I know that I will inherit it?"[319] Hashem answered his question by informing him about the future exile to Egypt."[320] This is because the experiences that Avraham's descendants were to endure in Egypt would spur them to an elevated level

---

315   *Ramban, Parashas Vayeira* 22:16.
316   *Maseches Shabbos* 97a.
317   Based on *Meshech Chochmah, Parashas Bo* 12:21.
318   *Midrash Tanchuma, Parashas Lech Lecha, perek* 9.
319   *Parashas Lech Lecha* 15:8.
320   *Parashas Lech Lecha* 15:13.

of faith. The merit of the faith that Avraham's descendants achieved in Egypt would be rewarded with the inheritance of Eretz Yisrael, and their status as the Chosen Nation.

Chazal convey that *ma'aseh avos siman l'banim* — the occurrences of the forefathers foretell the future occurrences of the descendants. This means that not only were the experiences that Avraham, Yitzchak, and Yaakov underwent replicated by their descendants, but also that their descendants replicated the spiritual achievements of the forefathers:

- Avraham was exiled to Egypt as a result of famine and he experienced miracles that allowed him and his wife, Sarah, to escape from the evil clutches of Pharaoh. After taking Sarah, Pharaoh was forced to set her free and he instructed Avraham and Sarah to leave the country. Avraham and Sara, emerged from Egypt with great wealth: cattle, silver, and gold.[321]
- Likewise, the descendants of Avraham and Sarah arrived in Egypt as a result of a famine and were held captive there. Finally, Hashem struck the Egyptians with ten plagues, which compelled Pharaoh to free the Jews. After the splitting of the Yam Suf, the nation of Yisrael emerged from Egypt, enriched with the loot of the Egyptians.[322]

This would be a recurrent theme in the aftermath of the Exodus. Many other seminal events experienced by our illustrious forefathers would be repeated by their descendants, as we will see in the coming chapters.

---

321 Ibid. 13:2.
322 *Ramban, Parashas Lech Lecha* 12:10.

SEVENTEEN

FOUR HUNDRED YEARS OF EXILE – TAPPING THE INNER EMUNAH

he Jewish People became an independent nation upon the Exodus from Egypt. Yaakov and his descendants entered Egypt as seventy individuals, corresponding to the seventy nations of the world, and they exited 210 years later as a nation of six hundred thousand males between the ages of twenty and sixty. During the years of their subjugation in Egypt, the Jewish nation was in the nascent stages of its emergence as a nation. In this embryonic phase of development, they were particularly vulnerable to the pernicious influence of their subjugators. The Egyptians were the most depraved and immoral nation on earth,[323] which put the Jewish People in an environment that was ripe for a precipitous downfall. In fact, they sunk to the very bottom of a spiritual abyss, the forty-ninth level of impurity.

The experiences of the Jewish People in Egypt mirrored that of their forefather Avraham:

- Avraham, the son of the idolater Terach, was born into the darkest of nations, the nation of Kasdim. Similarly, his descendants

---

323   *Toras Kohanim, Acharei Mos, perek* 9.

developed into a nation in the deep darkness of the spiritual impurity of Egypt.[324]

- Avraham emerged from the darkness and went on to illuminate the world with his faith. Likewise, B'nei Yisrael emerged from the darkness of Egypt and illuminated the world with the Torah they received on Mount Sinai.

Avraham was born into the deep darkness of the forty-ninth level of impurity, and it was not until the forty-ninth year of his life[325] that he reached full recognition of his Creator.[326] Likewise, the Jewish People in Egypt reached the forty-ninth level of impurity; the Exodus saved them from descending any further to the lowest level, from which there is no return. We recite in the Haggadah of *Pesach*, "If Hashem had not taken our fathers out of Egypt, we and our sons and our grandsons would still be enslaved in Egypt." If the Exodus would have been delayed any further it could not have happened at all, because they would have descended into the fiftieth level of impurity.[327]

Despite their descent into the depths of impurity, the Jewish People did not completely lose sight of their illustrious lineage, and they retained their identity as descendants of Avraham, Yitzchak, and Yaakov. They did not change their manner of dress or speech, nor did they engage in forbidden relations, or speak ill of their fellow Jews.[328] The faith that they inherited from Avraham never abandoned them, and although it may have been temporarily suppressed, it remained an integral part of their makeup.[329]

This lasting spark of faith allowed for a rapid ascent from the impurity

---

324   *Maharal Sefer Gevuras Hashem, perek* 5.

325   *Sefer Panim Yafos, Parashas Lech Lecha.* When Avraham was forty-eight years old he was in the forty-ninth year of his existence.

326   *Bereishis Rabbah* 64:4. The Talmud (*Nedarim* 32a) states he recognized his Creator at the age of three, however there are various degrees of his recognition of Hashem and he reached a more advanced recognition of Hashem at age forty-eight (*Kesef Mishnah, Hilchos Avodas Kochavim* 1:3).

327   *Chasam Sofer, Sefer Toras Moshe, Parashas Re'eh.*

328   *Mechilta, Parashas Bo, Parashah* 5.

329   *Meshech Chochmah, Parashas Bo* 12:21; *Chasam Sofer, Sefer Toras Moshe, Parashas Lech Lecha* 15:6.

that they found themselves in. In fact, Hashem pulled them out of all forty-nine levels of impurity in one great leap on the night of Pesach, as the Torah states,[330] "And I carried you on the wings of eagles and I brought you to me."[331] For Avraham, his ascent from impurity was by necessity a gradual one, but for his descendants a rapid ascent was possible. This was due to the latent sanctity that they harbored as a legacy of their descendancy from Avraham.

---

330   *Parashas Bo* 19:4.

331   *Chasam Sofer, Sefer Toras Moshe, Parashas Re'eh.*

FOLLOWING IN THE path of their fore-father Avraham, the Jewish People were exiled to Egypt. They were tainted spiritually by the depraved environment in Egypt, but the latent spirituality that they inherited from their forefathers never left them. Hashem pulled them out of the forty-nine level of impurity and their original purity was restored.

EIGHTEEN

THE MITZVAH OF KIDDUSH HA'CHODESH

O n the first day of the month of Nissan, Hashem said to Moshe, "This month shall be for you the first of the months."[332] The simple meaning of this statement is that Hashem established the month of Nissan as the first month of the year, with all of the other months to be counted from it, e.g., Iyar, the second month, and Sivan, the third month, etc. The deeper intent of this statement was to establish the mitzvah of *kiddush ha'chodesh*, the first mitzvah given to Yisrael as a nation.[333]

Why do we count Nissan as the first month of the year and not the month of Tishrei, which, according to the opinion of Rabbi Eliezer, was the first month after Creation?[334] In the Rosh Hashanah liturgy we recite, "This day was the conception of creation," which implies that we accept the opinion of Rabbi Eliezer that Tishrei is the first month.

In order to answer this, it would be helpful to start with some background on the Exodus of the Jewish People from Egypt. The *Ibn Ezra* maintains that the *mazalos* did not allow for the possibility of the Exodus from Egypt.[335] Hashem lifted the Jewish People above the *mazalos* prior to the Exodus, making them immune to the premonitions

---

332   *Parashas Bo* 19:4.
333   *Rashi*, ibid.
334   *Ran, Maseches Rosh Hashanah* 16a.
335   *Parashas Ki Sisa* 33:21.

of the *mazalos*. Since the natural world is subject to the *mazalos*, the transcendence of the Jewish People over the *mazalos* elevated them above the natural world. This new reality was tantamount to a new creation of the world, which made the month of Nissan, the month of the Exodus, the first month of this new world.

With this, the Jewish People were replicating the experiences of their forefather, Avraham:

- The *mazalos* did not allow for Avraham and Sarah to have children, but Hashem lifted Avraham above the stars to demonstrate that the premonitions of the *mazalos* would not prevent him from having children.[336] Hashem repositioned the star *tzeddek* from the west to the east to make it possible for Avraham to have children.[337]
- The *mazalos* did not allow the Exodus from Egypt. Hashem lifted the Jewish People above the *mazalos*, and they now transcended the *mazalos* and were no longer subject to their premonitions. The Jewish nation would be henceforth directly under Hashem and the *mazalos* would have no influence over them. However, this is only the case for events that occur to Yisrael as a nation, but individuals among the Jewish People remain under the *mazalos*, as the Talmud states that fertility, longevity, and income are not dependent on merit, but on *mazal*.[338]

The new status of the Jewish People is indicated by Hashem's statement to Moshe, "And I appeared to the Avos with *Kel Shakai* and the name of Hashem was not known to them."[339] Prior to the Exodus, Hashem guided the Jewish People with His name Kel Shakai, which implies that Hashem overrides the premonitions of the *mazalos*. This is what Hashem did for Avraham and Sarah to enable them to have children, and He continues to do so for individuals among the Jewish

---

336 *Rashi, Parashas Lech Lecha* 15:5.

337 *Maseches Shabbos* 156b.

338 *Maseches Mo'ed Katan* 28a.

339 *Parashas Va'eira* 6:3.

People. A Jewish individual is subject to the *mazalos*, but upon prayer and good deeds Hashem will override the *mazalos* for him. For the Jews as a nation however, Hashem guides them with His ineffable name of "Hashem," which implies that they are directly under Him and are not subject to the *mazalos* at all.

The concept that the Jewish People have been elevated over the natural world is symbolized by the mitzvah of *kiddush ha'chodesh*. This mitzvah is to sanctify the new month upon seeing the renewal of the moon, or, when that is not possible, according to calculations of when this renewal occurs. The mitzvah also includes *ibur hashanah*, the establishment of a leap year, when necessary, in order to ensure that the *mo'adim* (Jewish holidays) fall out in the correct season, i.e., Pesach in the spring and Sukkos in the fall.[340]

The Torah authorized the Sanhedrin (supreme Jewish court) in Jerusalem to calculate the expected appearance of the new moon and to establish Rosh Chodesh and the *mo'adim* on the basis of their calculations. Their authorization is complete; if the sages erred in their calculation of the new moon, even deliberately, the day that they establish is nevertheless regarded as Rosh Chodesh.[341] The day of Rosh Chodesh, despite being established in error, serves to determine natural events that depend on the lunar year! For example, Chazal relate that the signs of virginity of a girl under three years of age can reverse, but not if she is older than three. If a girl was born on the first day of the month, and the Sanhedrin erred in their calculations and added an extra day to the previous month, thus delaying the girl's third birthday, her signs of virginity are still reversible on the thirtieth day of the last month, even though by nature, the new moon already appeared, and she already turned three years old.[342] Thus, in essence, Chazal, through their ability to set Rosh Chodesh, have the power to alter the natural order of the world.

---

340 *Sefer HaChinuch.* This is in accordance with the *Rambam.* However, the *Ramban* is of the opinion that the mitzvah of the sanctification of the moon and the mitzvah of establishing a leap year are two separate mitzvos (*Sefer HaMitzvos*, mitzvah 153).

341 *Maseches Rosh Hashanah* 25a.

342 *Yerushalmi, Maseches Kesuvos* 1:2.

With this we can explain the reason why we recite *Hallel* on Rosh Chodesh. The recitation of *Hallel* normally commemorates a miracle — e.g., the miracle of the Exodus, the miracle of Chanukah — but what miracle occurred on Rosh Chodesh? Rabbi Mordechai Neugroschel suggests that Rosh Chodesh celebrates the miracle of the power of the the Sanhedrin to alter the order of the natural world, which is commemorated through the recital of *Hallel* on Rosh Chodesh.[343]

Similarly, says the *Chasam Sofer*, the decision of the Sanhedrin to establish a leap year is also a determinant of nature. The Torah commands us each year to read the section of the Torah that commands us not to forget the deeds of Amalek, because failing to mention the deeds of Amalek for a period of twelve months may cause us to forget their wicked deeds. Yet, when the Sanhedrin establishes a leap year, a period of thirteen months goes by without mentioning the deeds of Amalek. Nevertheless, we are not in danger of forgetting their deeds: Since the Torah sages decreed that thirteen months constitute a year, we are not susceptible to forgetting their deeds for the entire extended year, even though normally twelve months is considered the maximal time for remembering an event.[344]

The mitzvah of *kiddush ha'chodesh* thus reflects the concept that Yisrael, through the mitzvos, transcends the physical world. Moreover, the Torah, and by extension the Torah sages, are the determinants of natural events, and not the opposite.[345] This is because the Torah is the blueprint of creation; Hashem looked into the Torah and created the world.[346] This concept is strikingly illustrated in the authority given to the Sanhedrin with the mitzvah of *kiddush ha'chodesh*, the first mitzvah given to Yisrael as a nation.

---

343 *Sefer V'Hasheivosa El Levavecha.*
344 *Teshuvos Chasam Sofer, Even Ha'Ezer,* §119.
345 Rav Yehudah Copperman in *Iyunim B'Parshanut HaMikra.*
346 *Bereishis Rabbah* 1:1.

THE MITZVAH OF *kiddush ha'chodesh* symbolizes the concept that the Jewish People transcend the natural world. Prior to the Exodus, the Jewish People were lifted above the *mazalos*, which is what made the Exodus possible. This was tantamount to a new creation, which made Nissan the first month of this new world.

NINETEEN

THE MITZVOS OF BRIS MILAH AND KORBAN PESACH

P rior to their Exodus from Egypt, the Jewish People were given two critical mitzvos that provided them with the merits they needed to be redeemed: the mitzvos of *korban Pesach* and *bris milah,* the latter being a prerequisite for the former. Rabbi Masya ben Cheresh comments:

'I passed by and I saw and it was a time for love,'[347] it was time [for the fulfillment] of the vow that Hashem made to Avraham to redeem his children, and [the Jewish People] did not have in their hands mitzvos to occupy themselves with in order to merit redemption, as the Torah states, 'And you were naked and bare.'[348] And He gave them two mitzvos, the blood of Pesach and the blood of milah, as they performed the bris milah on that night, as the Torah states, 'And you were rolling in your blood,'[349] — two bloods, the blood of Pesach and the blood of milah.[350]

Blood symbolizes self-sacrifice. The two "blood mitzvos" of *bris milah* and *korban Pesach,* epitomize the concept of self-sacrifice for Hashem.

---

347   *Sefer Yechezkel* 16:8.
348   Ibid, *pasuk* 7.
349   Ibid, *pasuk* 6.
350   *Mechilta, Parashas Bo.*

Throughout the generations, the Jewish People have been willing to give up their lives to keep these two mitzvos. This can be seen from the statement of the Talmud quoted earlier: "Any *mitzvah* for which Yisrael have been willing to give up their life at a time of persecution, such as *avodah zarah* and *milah*, remains strong in their hands."[351] The source for the self-sacrifice of the Jewish People lies in their foundation: they follow in the path blazed for them by their forefather Avraham. Avraham demonstrated his willingness to give up his life for Hashem in order to fulfill the mitzvah of *bris milah*, and his descendants do the same.

With regard to idolatry as well, Avraham famously offered up his life to avoid transgressing when Nimrod threw him into a fiery furnace for his rejection of his father's idols.[352] The mitzvah of *korban Pesach* symbolizes self-sacrifice for idolatry. The Jewish People were steeped in idolatry in Egypt,[353] and the Egyptians worshipped the *mazalos*, particularly the *mazal* of the lamb, which was at its zenith in the month of Nissan. When Hashem commanded B'nei Yisrael in the mitzvah of *korban Pesach*, He instructed them to "withdraw and take for yourselves a sheep,"[354] which implies that they shall withdraw their hands from their idols and instead designate a lamb for a *korban Pesach*.[355] Thus, the act of designating and bringing a lamb for the *korban Pesach* was a renouncement of their heretical beliefs in the power of the *mazalos*.

The designation of a lamb in Egypt for the *korban Pesach* was an act of great self-sacrifice. The Jewish People risked their lives when they took a lamb — the object of Egyptian idol worship — and tied it to the bed-post for four days, and then slaughtered and ate it. With the very public designation of a lamb as a *korban Pesach*, the Jewish People were following the path of their forefather Avraham and putting their lives on the line for the sake of their rejection of idolatry.

---

351   *Maseches Shabbos* 130a.

352   *Bereishis Rabbah* 38:11.

353   *Rashi* states that when the Jewish People stood in front of the Yam Suf, the Satan argued that Hashem should not save them because the Jewish People were no different from the Egyptians, as both nations worshipped *avodah zarah*.

354   *Parashas Bo* 12:21.

355   *Mechilta*, ibid.

The *Chasam Sofer* maintains that the Egyptians celebrated the rise of the *mazal* by bringing sacrifices to it on the fourteenth of the month of Nissan. They started preparing for this celebration a few days prior to the fourteenth by seeking out appropriate items to be brought as sacrifices. Yisrael's actions in bringing the *korban Pesach* paralleled and countered the Egyptians'; while the Egyptians occupied themselves for several days making purchases for the sacrifice to the *mazal* of the lamb in their belief in its primacy, B'nei Yisrael were busy taking a lamb to be brought as a sacrifice to Hashem. With the very public designation of a lamb as a *korban Pesach*, the Jewish People were proclaiming that the *mazal* of the lamb is subservient to Hashem, Who is the sole power of the world. Moreover, the slaughtering of the lamb for the *korban Pesach*, at a time when the *mazal* of the lamb was at the height of its "power," signified that the *mazalos* had no influence over the Jewish nation.

However, as we said, only Yisrael as a nation transcends the *mazalos*, but not as individuals. The Jewish People are only considered a nation when they are united; when they are fragmented and in disunity, they are no more than a group of individuals.[356] Since the *korban Pesach* symbolized Yisrael's ascendancy over the *mazalos*, it was important that it be eaten in a manner that reflected their nation-status. Thus, an integral component of the *korban Pesach* was that it was eaten in a group, and an individual was not allowed to separate himself from the group to eat alone,[357] as the Torah states, "It shall be eaten in one house; the flesh shall not be taken out of the house."[358] When the Jewish People came together to fulfill the mitzvah of *korban Pesach*, they demonstrated that their strength as a nation lies in their unity.

This seminal moment in Yisrael's birth as a nation, the taking of the *korban Pesach*, does not emerge from a vacuum. One can hear the echoes of Avraham's earlier footsteps. The contrast between B'nei Yisrael's demonstrations of faith surrounding the taking of the lamb as a *korban*, and the Egyptian rituals surrounding the lamb as a *mazal*, is reminiscent

---

356   *Sichos Mussar, Parashas Mishpatim,* year 5731.
357   *Rambam, Hilchos Korban Pesach* 9:1 and *Kesef Mishnah.*
358   Ibid, *pasuk* 46.

of Avraham and his public battle with the generation of the *Haflagah*. The generation of the *Haflagah* believed that Hashem had given the world over to the *mazalos*, while Avraham openly proclaimed that Hashem is the sole Power in the world and that He had not abdicated His rule in any way.[359] Similarly, by taking a lamb for a *korban Pesach*, the Jewish People were publicly showing their contempt for the heretical beliefs of the Egyptians, and were proclaiming to all that the lamb, like every *mazal*, is no more than a tool in the hands of Hashem. Thus, once more we see that Avraham's accomplishments were passed on to his children, who through their own actions, acquired them as their own.

---

359   Rabbeinu Bachya, *Parashas Vayeira* 22:1.

HASHEM GAVE THE Jewish People two important mitzvos in Egypt: the mitzvos of *bris milah* and *korban Pesach*. These mitzvos gave the Jewish People the merit they needed for their upcoming Exodus from Egypt. The Jewish People fulfilled these mitzvos with self-sacrifice for Hashem, just as Avraham had done many years prior.

TWENTY

KRIAS YAM SUF

pon experiencing the miracles of Hashem in Egypt, B'nei Yisrael reached great heights of faith in Hashem. They exhibited this faith when they went out of Egypt into the desert without the means to survive, relying purely on their faith in Hashem, as Yirmiyahu the prophet said, "I remember the *chessed* of your youth, the love of your nuptials; you followed after me into the desert into an uncultivated land."[360] They put their complete faith in Hashem to provide for them, and followed after Him into the barren desert.

With this, the Jewish People were treading in the path of their forefather Avraham, who exhibited the same great faith in Hashem when he left his previous life behind and traveled to an unknown, unidentified land. Hashem instructed Avraham, "Go forth from your land and your birthplace and from the house of your father to the land that I will show you."[361] The *Ramban* explains that Hashem did not immediately divulge to Avraham his ultimate destination. Avraham wandered from one land to another, and from one kingdom to another, without knowing his destination, until he finally arrived in Eretz Canaan. Only then did Hashem inform him that this was the land that would be given to his children.[362] Similarly, the Jewish People traveled from place to place in the desert without knowing in advance where they were going. Although they knew

---

360 *Sefer Yirmiyahu* 2:2.
361 *Parashas Lech Lecha* 12:1.
362 *Ramban, Parashas Lech Lecha* 12:1.

that their ultimate destination was Eretz Yisrael, the time to enter the Land was not yet ripe, and they wandered in the desert for more than a year.[363] They did not commence their travels to Eretz Yisrael until Iyar of the second year, fourteen months after the Exodus from Egypt.[364]

Despite the great level of faith in Hashem that the Jewish People achieved in Egypt, they were still lacking an important aspect of faith — faith in the prophecy of Moshe. This faith was an essential prerequisite for receiving the Torah, as the vast majority of the Torah would be heard from Moshe, and not directly from Hashem. The Jewish People would hear only two of the ten commandments from Hashem; the remaining 611 mitzvos would be heard from Moshe. Furthermore, the Oral Torah was heard exclusively from Moshe, and without the Oral Torah, it is impossible to arrive at a proper understanding of even one mitzvah of the Torah.[365] Thus, the Torah is called *Toras Moshe*, as the prophet said, "Remember the Torah of My servant Moshe."[366]

At the Yam Suf, B'nei Yisrael were presented with a challenge that would enable them to attain this high level of faith. Much as their forefather Yitzchak had demonstrated this level of faith by his willingness to follow Avraham to the *Akeidah*, B'nei Yisrael rose to the challenge and heeded Moshe's instructions to enter the sea. Defying the rational, they jumped into the Yam Suf and walked on into the deep water. Just like the *Akeidah*, when Yitzchak was reprieved at what seemed to be the last moment, the waters split when they reached the people's noses, and they continued on dry land.[367] With the splitting of the Yam Suf, their faith in prophecy was reinforced, as the Torah testifies:[368] "And they believed in Hashem and in Moshe his servant."[369]

---

363   *Malbim, Parashas Beshalach* 13:17.

364   If not for the sin of the Spies, they would have entered Eretz Yisrael at that time, but ultimately, they wandered in the desert for another thirty-nine years before finally entering Eretz Yisrael.

365   *Hakdamah* to *Sefer Ha'flaah* on *Maseches Kesuvos, Pischah Zeira.*

366   *Sefer Malachi* 3:22.

367   *Shemos Rabbah, Parashas Beshalach* 21:10.

368   *Parashas Beshalach* 14:31.

369   See *Sefer Meshech Chochmah, Parashas Beshalach* 14:15; *Sefer Panim Yafos, Parashas Beshalach* 14:31. Although Chazal teach us that *Shevet Yehudah* merited the kingship because Nachshon ben Aminadav from *Shevet Yehudah* was the first to jump into the Yam Suf, the *Sefer Yefei To'ar* explains that after Nachshon jumped in, the rest of Klal Yisrael followed his lead and jumped in as well.

THE JEWISH PEOPLE followed Moshe into the desert without knowing their destination, in the same way that Avraham traveled away from his homeland at Hashem's directive without knowing his destination. At the Yam Suf, the Jewish People put their faith in Moshe and jumped into the sea even before it split, just as Yitzchak put his faith in Avraham and allowed himself to be led to the *Akeidah*.

TWENTY-ONE

MILCHEMES AMALEK

As the Jewish People came closer to the ultimate achievement of receiving the Torah and forming a union with Hashem, they were forced to confront the people who stood in their way — the nation of Amalek. Amalek descends from Eisav, and Eisav's resentment of Yaakov is everlasting, as *Rashi* teaches:[370] "It is a halachah that Eisav hates Yaakov."[371]

Eisav reaps a tangible benefit from persecuting the Jewish People. Although Eisav forfeited Yitzchak's blessings to Yaakov, he was assured by his father that "when [Yaakov] goes down, you will remove his yoke from your neck."[372] As we saw, this means that the blessings were given to Yaakov conditionally, so if he (or his descendants) stray from the path of Torah, the blessings will be taken away and given to Eisav instead. Since the destinies of Eisav and Yaakov are forever linked, when the Jewish nation suffers a spiritual downturn, it is to the benefit of the descendants of Eisav.[373] Consequently, the people of Amalek, as descendants of Eisav, have a special interest in impeding the spiritual growth of Yisrael and preventing them from following the path of the Torah.

The Jewish People are distinguished by their faith — the awareness that Hashem controls nature like a hammer in the hands of the

---

370 *Rashi, Parashas Vayishlach* 33:4.
371 *Malbim, Parashas Beshalach* 17:8.
372 *Parashas Toldos* 27:40.
373 *Maseches Megillah* 6a.

blacksmith. The *Netziv* explains that in contrast to the Jewish People, Amalek espoused the belief that nature is an independent force that is not controlled by Hashem. Amalek attacked B'nei Yisrael in the desert in an attempt to inculcate them with this perverse belief.[374]

The Jewish nation went out to battle with Amalek to fight off their pernicious influence. The Torah states that Moshe raised his hands heavenward "with faith" until the setting of the sun.[375] By raising his hands toward the sun, Moshe was directing B'nei Yisrael toward the belief that nature is in the hands of Hashem.[376] B'nei Yisrael managed to strengthen themselves in their faith and this gave them the impetus to defeat Amalek in battle.

The Torah states, "Hashem vows that His name and His Throne are not complete until the name of Amalek is wiped out.[377] The *Netziv* explains that the world was created with the first two letters of the Ineffable Four-Letter Name of Hashem, the *yud* and the *hei*; the next world was created with the *yud* and this world was created with the *hei*. Hashem rules over these worlds with the last two letters of His Name, the *vav* and the *hei*. The letter *vav* signifies Hashem's rule over the upper spheres, while the second *hei* of His Name signifies the Divine Providence in this World, manifested through the routine works of nature. These four letters come together in Hashem's Name, which indicates that Hashem not only created the world, but also runs the world after its creation.

Amalek, in its denial of Divine Providence and its heretical belief of nature as an independent force, seeks to separate the first two letters of His Name — which indicate the creation of this world and the next — from the last two letters, which indicate His rule over the worlds. This demonstrated their belief that Hashem abdicated His rule over the world after He created it. Thus, as long as Amalek exists, the Name of Hashem is not complete.[378]

---

374 *Sefer Ha'amek Davar, Parashas Beshalach* 17:16.
375 *Parashas Beshalach* 17:12.
376 *Sefer Ha'amek Davar*, ibid. 17:14.
377 *Parashas Beshalach* 17:16.
378 *Sefer Ha'amek Davar*, ibid.

The Torah tells us that Yehoshua bin Nun weakened Amalek with his sword. Why did he not finish the job and destroy it completely? Amalek is the physical manifestation of the administering angel Samael, who makes it his task to plant seeds of doubt in the faith of the Jewish nation.[379] Destroying the nation of Amalek without destroying what they represent — the heretical belief that nature is an independent force — is pointless because the angel Samael will simply manifest itself in some other form. At the time of the war with Amalek, the Jewish nation had not strengthened themselves sufficiently in their faith to completely wipe out this heretical belief, and thus, complete destruction of Amalek was not yet possible. Nevertheless, with the weakening of Amalek at the hands of Yehoshua, the Jewish People's belief in Divine Providence was reinforced.

---

379   *Alshich HaKadosh, Parashas Beshalach.*

THE NATION OF Amalek descends from Eisav and inherited his resentment for the Jewish People. Amalek makes it their job to persecute the Jewish People and contaminate them with the heretical belief of nature as an independent source. Strengthening ourselves in our faith in Divine Providence is the only defense against the pernicious influence of Amalek.

TWENTY-TWO

MARAH

On the way to Mount Sinai, the Jewish People traveled for three days in the desert without water until they reached Marah, where they found the water too bitter to drink. Hashem showed Moshe an "*eitz*," and he threw it into the water and it was sweetened.[380] The Talmud explains that the water is a reference to Torah — they had traveled for three days without learning Torah.[381]

In order to rectify this, they were given three sections of the Torah to occupy themselves with: Shabbos, *parah adumah*, and *dinim*.[382] These three mitzvos are representative of the three categories of mitzvos that would soon be given on Mount Sinai: *chukim, eidos,* and *mishpatim:*[383]

- *Chukim* are the mitzvos whose underlying logic is hidden from human understanding.
- *Eidos* are the mitzvos that commemorate the great ways of Hashem in the world.
- *Mishpatim* are the mitzvos that logic would dictate even if Hashem had not commanded them.

---

380 *Parashas Beshalach* 15:22–23.
381 *Maseches Bava Kama* 82a.
382 *Rashi, Parashas Beshalach* 15:25. However, the Talmud in *Sanhedrin* states that they were given the mitzvos of Shabbos, *kibud av v'eim*, and *dinim*.
383 *Maharal, Gur Aryeh, Parashas Beshalach* 15:25.

The three mitzvos given at Marah fall into these three categories of mitzvos:

- *Parah adumah* is a *chok*. It is the ultimate *chok* because it is a mitzvah that completely defies logic: it purifies the impure while also causing the pure to become impure.[384]
- Shabbos is in the category of *eidos* because it commemorates the Creation of the world, as the Torah states: "Because for six days Hashem made the heavens and the earth, the sea, and everything in it, and He rested on the seventh day; therefore Hashem blessed the day of Shabbos and He sanctified it."[385]
- *Dinim* fits into the category of *mishpatim* because the mitzvah has us setting up a justice system, which is a mitzvah with a very apparent logic, as the Mishnah states: "If not for the fear of the government, man would swallow up his friend alive."[386]

These three sections of the Torah were given in Marah in order to expose B'nei Yisrael to the diverse types of mitzvos in the Torah, as a prelude to receiving the Torah at Mount Sinai.[387] Until that point, the mitzvos that Hashem had given to the Jewish People fell into the category of *mishpatim* and *eidos*, but not *chukim*. At Marah, B'nei Yisrael were given their first exposure to the *chukim* in order to pave the way for their eventual acceptance of all the mitzvos of the Torah. The grouping together of these three mitzvos taught the Jewish People that they must be equally accepting of all three categories of mitzvos. It was important for the Jewish People to receive the *chukim*, despite their inability to comprehend them, with the same wholehearted acceptance as the other categories of Torah mitzvos. The ability to comprehend the underlying reasons for the mitzvos should have no bearing on their acceptance; faith in Hashem alone should be the foundation for the Torah's acceptance. This realization was a critical prerequisite for *Matan Torah*.

---

384   *Rashi, Maseches Niddah* 9a.
385   *Parashas Yisro* 20:11.
386   *Pirkei Avos* 3:2.
387   *Seforno, Kli Yakar.*

In essence, there is little difference between the various types of mitzvos, as the true reasons for all the mitzvos — even the *mishpatim* — are beyond human comprehension. The perceived reasons for the *mishpatim* that seem so apparent may not be their primary purpose, and there may be other reasons for those mitzvos that we are unable to fathom.[388] Moreover, there are numerous details to every mitzvah, and even when the rationale for the mitzvah seems straightforward, the reason behind some of the details of the mitzvah may remain obscured. Yisrael's approach to the *mishpatim* should be similar to that of the *chukim* — all mitzvos should be kept only because Hashem commanded them, and not because of any presumed reason for a particular mitzvah. Thus, the Torah states: "Honor your father and mother as Hashem your G-d commanded you."[389] Although the mitzvah of honoring parents seems to have a clear and obvious rationale, nevertheless, the mitzvah shall be fulfilled because Hashem commanded it, and not as a result of any deductive reasoning.[390]

Notably, however, although one may not make his understanding of the mitzvah a precondition for its fulfillment, once one has committed himself to keeping all of the mitzvos unconditionally, he may use his wisdom to try to discover the reasons behind them.[391] Rav Pinchas Horowitz maintains that the rationale behind the mitzvos would not always remain beyond human comprehension; with a wholehearted

---

388   *Kli Yakar, Parashas Va'eschanan* 4:8.

389   *Parashas Va'eschanan* 5:16.

390   *Aruch HaShulchan, Yoreh De'ah* 20:2.

391   *Chasam Sofer* on the *Haggadah Shel Pesach*. The *Chasam Sofer* uses this concept to explain the distinction between the wise son and the wicked son. On the surface, their queries seem similar. The wise son asks, "What are the *eidos, chukim,* and *mishpatim* that Hashem our G-d commanded you," while the wicked son asks, "What is this *avodah* to you." The *Chasam Sofer* explains that the wicked son mentions "this *avodah*," i.e., the *avodah* of the *korban Pesach*, which is the mitzvah of the day. His desire to understand the mitzvah is not theoretical; he preconditions his acceptance of the mitzvah on this understanding. If the answer to his question does not please him, he simply will not do the mitzvah. The question of the wise son, on the other hand, is not specifically about the mitzvah of the *korban Pesach*, it is relevant to the mitzvos in general. Since he already demonstrated his unconditional acceptance of Hashem and His Word, and is not asking about the mitzvah of the day, his question is academic, indicating that although he would like to comprehend the mitzvah, his performance of the mitzvah is immaterial to his comprehension. See also *Beis HaLevi, Parashas Bo*.

acceptance of the mitzvos, as occurred on Mount Sinai, the underlying logic of the mitzvos would eventually come into clearer focus. This was symbolized by the bitter water in Marah that was sweetened when Moshe threw an *eitz* into the water. The bitter water symbolizes the mitzvos that are difficult to understand and thus are "bitter" to the palate. The *eitz* that Moshe threw into the water symbolized the Torah, which is an *eitz ha'chaim* — a tree of life. This teaches us that with the wholehearted acceptance of all the mitzvos of the Torah, those that initially seem incomprehensible will eventually become "sweetened" and the underlying reason accessible.[392]

Furthermore, the *eitz ha'chaim* that Moshe used to sweeten the water symbolized that with their upcoming acceptance of the Torah on Mount Sinai, the Jewish People would complete the correction of Adam's sin.[393] As we said, Avraham rectified Adam's sin when he successfully passed the test of the *Akeidah*, but it was imperative that Yisrael, as a nation, correct it as well. As we mentioned in the first section, the *Eitz HaDaas* was not intended to be forbidden forever; if Adam had abstained from eating from it until the onset of Shabbos, it would have become permitted.[394] The power of Adam's faith, demonstrated by his adherence to the word of Hashem, could have sweetened the tree so that it would have become one with its twin tree, the *Eitz HaChaim*, which was a source of eternal life. Similarly, the waters of Marah, which represent the Torah, were bitter, and could not sustain life. But with the strength of Yisrael's faith, demonstrated by their wholehearted acceptance of all categories of mitzvos, the waters could be transformed by the *eitz hachaim* and become potable and the source of life.

---

392   *Sefer Panim Yafos, Parashas Beshalach*, see also *Kli Yakar*.
393   *Sefer Panim Yafos.*
394   *Sefer Daas Tevunos*, also *Chasam Sofer, Sefer Toras Moshe, Parashas Bereishis.*

IN MARAH, THE Jewish People were given three mitzvos that represented the three categories of mitzvos: *chukim, eidos,* and *mishpatim.* The lesson of Marah is that the three categories of mitzvos are in essence one and the same. The mitzvos of all three categories should be accepted out of faith in Hashem and not out of any perceived reason for them.

AFTERWORD

O ur forefathers' faith in Hashem was an indelible part of their essence, so much so that they were able to pass it on to their descendants, making the nation of Yisrael *ma'aminim b'nei ma'aminim*.[395] However, Yisrael's descendancy from their great forefathers only ensured that they possessed the raw genetic material that allowed them to carry on in their ways; it did not guarantee that they would actually achieve this. In this section we saw how the nation Yisrael, through actions that uncannily mirrored those of their fathers, actualized the potential within them. They emerged from the darkest, lowest level of impurity, like Avraham, and they ushered in a new world in which the supernatural was supreme. Like Yitzchak, they demonstrated their faith that Hashem transmits His word through the prophets. And they accepted the mitzvos as Hashem's commandment, irrespective of their own understanding. Adam and Chavah's sins were finally rectified, not just in potential, but in action. The Jewish People were now ready to receive the Torah.

---

395   *Maseches Shabbos* 97a.

MA'AMAD HAR SINAI

At the time that Hashem revealed Himself
to give the Torah to Yisrael, He gave
to Moshe, in order, the Mikra, Mishnah,
Talmud, and Aggadah, as the Torah states:
"And Hashem spoke all of these words,"
even what a student would ask his rav,
Hashem told over to Moshe at that time.
(Shemos Rabbah 47:1)

Introduction to Stage VI

fter the Jewish People proved their faith in Hashem and His prophet, Moshe, they now embarked on a gradual ascension of the spiritual ladder, one rung at a time. In this too, they followed the path of their forefather Avraham, who after climbing out of the forty-nine levels of impurity by the age of forty-eight, ascended the spiritual ladder of purity, one stage at a time until he reached the fiftieth level, at the age of ninety-nine.

Similarly, after B'nei Yisrael were pulled out of the forty-nine levels of impurity, they began their ascent to the fiftieth level of purity, which would make them fit to receive the Torah on Mount Sinai. This ascent started immediately upon the Exodus from Egypt, and culminated fifty days later with *Matan Torah*. Each day they ascended one rung of the ladder of spiritual purity, until they reached the ultimate level of purity, and were ready to receive the Torah.[396]

At Mount Sinai, Hashem told the Jewish People that they would be a "kingdom of *Kohanim* (priests) and a holy nation."[397] How would they become a kingdom of *Kohanim*? We mentioned previously that Avraham had taken over as High Priest from Shem because of his higher level of faith — his recognition that nature is no less a miracle than the supernatural. At Mount Sinai, all of Yisrael would reach this level, when Hashem stilled nature and the Jewish People witnessed with their own

---

396 *Maseches Pesachim* 3b.
397 *Parashas Yisro* 19:6.

eyes that there is nothing in the world but Hashem.[398] Although there could be only one High Priest, at *Matan Torah,* all Jewish People would become qualified to be *Kohanim.* Every Jewish person would perceive the hand of Hashem orchestrating nature with the same clarity as their forefather Avraham.

---

398 *Shemos Rabbah* 29:9.

TWENTY-THREE

UNITY OF PURPOSE

A s Yisrael traveled from Egypt toward the Sinai Desert, overcoming challenges such as the war with Amalek and the lack of water in Marah, they came together as a cohesive nation. *Rashi* relates that the nation of Yisrael arrived at Har Sinai, "like one man with one heart,"[399] with complete unity of purpose.[400] Unity was the last missing piece needed for *Matan Torah*, as the midrash states: "Hashem said, 'Since you hate discord and love peace and you camped out as one, this is the time that I will give you the Torah.'"[401]

The unity achieved at the foothills of Mount Sinai was an outgrowth of Yisrael's great humility, which enabled them to completely forego their identities as individuals and to focus instead on each person's standing within the community, as one piece of a whole.[402] Humility is a quality that is inherent to the Jewish People, as the Torah states: "It is not because you are the most numerous of the nations that Hashem desired you and chose you, because you are the least among the nations."[403] *Rashi* explains that Hashem desires Yisrael because they do not lift themselves up when Hashem bestows good on them, but

---

399   *Rashi, Parashas Yisro* 19:2.
400   *Sefer Derush Al HaTorah.*
401   *Rashi, Parashas Yisro* 19:2.
402   *Kli Yakar, Parashas Yisro* 19:2, Sichos Mussar, maamar 4, 5732.
403   *Parashas Va'eschanan* 7:7.

163

rather, they diminish themselves.[404] The trait of modesty is a legacy from Avraham, who commented, "I am but dirt and ashes."[405] As stated, it was his great humility and self-effacement that gave Avraham the ability to experience a profound recognition of Hashem. Likewise, it was the humility of Yisrael that made them fit to receive the Torah at Mount Sinai.

Achieving unity was a crucial prerequisite for receiving the Torah because the Torah can only be given to a nation, not to individuals, even to individuals as great as Avraham, Yitzchak, and Yaakov.[406] When there is discord among the people, they cannot be regarded as one united nation, but rather, as a collection of individuals. When Yisrael acted with one heart and helped each other set up camp, they were no longer an assortment of individuals, but a unified nation ready to receive the Torah.

The Torah could only be given to a unified nation because *Matan Torah* was tantamount to a marriage between Hashem and Yisrael, as *Rashi* states that Hashem went toward Yisrael at Mount Sinai like a groom going out toward his bride.[407] The nature of the union between Hashem and Yisrael is an everlasting one: Unlike a marriage between a man and a woman that can (sadly) end in divorce, the union between Hashem and Yisrael can never be broken.[408] An everlasting union is only possible with a nation, not with individuals, no matter how great, because no individual is guaranteed to remain pure and thus deserving of an eternal covenant with Hashem. The Talmud tells us that Yochanan was *Kohen Gadol* for seventy years but eventually became a *tzeduki* — a heretic who believed only in the Written Torah, not the Oral Torah.[409]

However, the Jewish People as a nation are guaranteed to remain pure. As we saw, Avraham expressed his concern that his descendants would sin and lose their status as the favored son of Hashem. Hashem

---

404   *Rashi*, ibid.
405   *Parashas Vayeira* 18:27.
406   Rabbeinu Bachya 46:27.
407   *Rashi, Parashas Yisro* 19:17.
408   *Maharal, Sefer Netzach Yisrael, perek* 47.
409   *Maseches Berachos* 29a.

answered, "Take for me a calf."[410] *Rashi* explains that Hashem's answer to Avraham meant that even if Yisrael sins, they would regain Hashem's favor by bringing sacrifices on the *Mizbei'ach,* which would atone for their sins.[411] Although an individual can also find atonement for his sins, if an individual Jew chooses to forego his atonement and distance himself from Hashem, He allows him to do so. This is not the case for the Jewish People as a nation. If they don't take their own initiative to repent and bring themselves closer to Hashem, He will coerce them into repentance. Hashem will not allow the Jewish nation to remain sullied by their sins.

The Jewish nation wanted to throw off the yoke of Hashem after the destruction of the first Beis Hamikdash, out of the mistaken belief that Hashem had expelled them from under His direct Divine Providence. Yechezkel responded with the prophecy: "I swear that I will rule over you with a strong hand and with an outstretched arm and with outpoured wrath." [412] Meaning that Hashem will never allow the Jewish People to abandon Him; instead Hashem will afflict them and force them to repent.[413]

This is confirmed in the Talmud, according to the opinion of Rabbi Yehoshua.[414]

> Rabbi Eliezer said, "If Yisrael repents they will be redeemed, and if not, they will not be redeemed. Rabbi Yehoshua asked, "If they don't repent, they won't be redeemed? Instead, Hashem will inflict on them a king whose decrees are harsh like those of Haman, and Yisrael will repent."[415]

The *Maharal* explains that for the Jewish People, even a forced repentance is meaningful and removes the taint of sin. This is because when

---

410 *Parashas Lech Lecha* 15:9.
411 Ibid. 15:6.
412 *Sefer Yechezkel* 20:32.
413 *Midrash Tanchuma, Parashas Nitzavim.*
414 The opinion of Rabbi Yehoshua generally prevails over that of Rabbi Eliezer.
415 *Maseches Sanhedrin* 97b.

the Jewish People sin, their essence remains unchanged; the purity of their souls can become temporarily obscured by the taint of their sins, but it can never disappear entirely. Even those who live a life of sin remain pure in their essence and when they repent, even if by force, their latent purity is restored.[416]

---

416 *Sefer Netzach Yisrael, perek* 11.

THE TORAH COULD only be given to the Jewish People as a unified nation because Hashem only gives the Torah to a nation, not to an individual. When the Jewish People are fragmented and in disunity, they are no more than a collection of individuals. When the Jewish People reached Mount Sinai, they came together as a unified nation, which made them fit to receive the Torah.

TWENTY-FOUR

NAASEH V'NISHMA

When Hashem offered them the Torah, the Jewish People famously declared, "We will do and we will hear."[417] They committed themselves to keeping the mitzvos of the Torah even without prior knowledge of the contents. Why did Hashem ask Yisrael to accept the Torah without first revealing to them the 613 mitzvos that it contained? Surely the Jewish People would not have rejected the Torah if Hashem had revealed the mitzvos to them prior to offering them the Torah. At Marah, the Jewish People had already demonstrated their willingness to keep all three categories of mitzvos, including the *chukim*, which are not comprehensible to the human mind.

Hashem did not reveal the 613 mitzvos prior to offering the Torah to Yisrael because the acceptance of all 613 mitzvos is not the same as an acceptance of the Torah as a whole. The Torah consists of an intricate web of mitzvos that makes up its great tapestry. Indeed, says Rav Avraham Kramer, brother of the Vilna Gaon,[418] every word of the Torah contains a mitzvah. The 613 mitzvos of the Torah are categories that encompass many other mitzvos as subcategories. Thus, even if Hashem would have forewarned the Jewish People of all 613 mitzvos of the Torah, it would not have done justice to the Torah. The Jewish People first needed to receive the Torah in order to gain a true sense of its contents.

---

417 *Parashas Mishpatim* 24:7.
418 *Sefer Ma'alos HaTorah, perek* 1.

Furthermore, the Torah encompasses more than just the mitzvos; the Torah is a spiritual guide for life. It includes the tractate of *Avos* that guides our behavior in this world. Thus, the acceptance of the mitzvos is not sufficient; the recipients must be willing to act in the manner that the Torah prescribes, as Chazal tell us, "*Derech eretz* (the code of proper conduct) precedes the Torah."[419]

With this, we can understand the refusal of the nations of the world to accept the Torah when it was offered to them:[420]

- The descendants of Eisav refused the Torah on the grounds that they were incapable of adhering to the prohibition of murder.
- The nation of Yishmael refused to accept the Torah because they found it impossible to keep the prohibition of theft.
- The nation of Amon refused to accept the Torah because the challenge of abstaining from forbidden relations was too much for them.

Why were these prohibitions grounds for these nations' refusal to accept the Torah? These prohibitions were not new! The prohibitions of murder, theft, and forbidden relations are included in the Seven Noachide Laws and are obligatory on all people at all times, irrespective of their willingness to accept the Torah!

The answer to this question is that the mitzvos given prior to *Matan Torah*, such as the Seven Noachide Laws, were given as individual mitzvos that included nothing more than the actual mitzvah. As part of the Torah, however, these mitzvos are broad categories that include many sub-mitzvos. For example, the prohibition of murder also includes the prohibition of shaming a person publicly, which is like killing him.[421] The prohibition of theft includes borrowing an item without permission, cheating someone out of his money,[422] or

---

419 *Vayikra Rabbah, perek* 9.
420 *Sifri, Ve'zos HaBerachah* §343
421 *Maseches Bava Metzia* 58b.
422 *Maseches Bava Metzia* 60b.

deceiving a person even if no loss is incurred.[423] This was too much for the nation of Yishmael to accept.

Furthermore, the mitzvos of the Torah are more than just mitzvos; they are a way of life. The midrash illustrates that when the non-Jewish nations rejected the Torah, they did so on the grounds that it impeded their way of life. The nation of Eisav did not just say that they could not adhere to the prohibition of murder, rather, they said, "[Eisav] was blessed by [Yitzchak], 'By your sword you shall live.'[424] We are unable to fulfill it." Meaning, the Torah demands more than just adherence to the mitzvos; it demands that its adherents conform their lifestyle and code of conduct to the way of the Torah. A Torah Jew does not just adhere to the prohibition of murder, he abhors the act and distances himself from it in every way. For the nation of Eisav, even if they do not actually commit murder, violence is an integral part of their way of life. They carry weapons and act violently, even when they do not actually kill anyone.

Similarly, for the the nation of Yishmael, theft is a way of life. They responded to Hashem's offer of the Torah, "Master of the world, the essence of Yishmael is to be a thief, as it states, 'And he will be a wild man; his hand will be in everything.' We cannot keep this prohibition."[425] Meaning, theft for the nation of Yishmael is a vocation and an integral part of their life. Even when they do not actually pilfer from their friends, they cheat their friends out of their money. For a Torah Jew, one must be as careful with another person's money as he is with his own.

The nations of Amon and Moav said, "Our very existence is due to the illicit relationship of Lot with his daughters; we can't keep the prohibition of forbidden relations." For Torah Jews, keeping their distance from forbidden relationships is the essence of sanctity and an important part of their service of Hashem. They distance themselves from even a small taint of this sin, as the midrash states: "The Holy One

---

423   *Tosefta, Bava Kama* 3:7.
424   *Parashas Toldos* 27:40.
425   *Parashas Vayeira* 16:12.

Blessed Be He says, "Don't say that it is only forbidden to have relations with a [forbidden] woman, but I can hold her, or hug her or kiss her without sin; one may not touch a [forbidden] woman at all."[426] For the nation of Amon and Moav, this kind of lifestyle is out of reach.

---

426   *Shir HaShirim Rabbah* 1:2, brought in *Mesilas Yesharim, perek* 11.

HASHEM OFFERED THE Torah to all the nations before offering it to Yisrael. The other nations were not prepared to accept the Torah because they found they were unsuited to adhere to it. In contrast, the Jewish People accepted the 613 mitzvos of the Torah without prior knowledge of its contents. They were more than happy to not only adhere to the mitzvos of the Torah, but also to conform their lifestyle to the Torah.

TWENTY-FIVE

THE ORAL TORAH

The Torah consists of both the Written and Oral Torah. The Written Torah encompasses the entire Torah, but without the Oral Torah that explains and elucidates it, the wisdom beneath the surface remains hidden and inaccessible.[427] Nevertheless, even on a superficial level, the Written Torah stands on its own. Every word in the Torah can be understood in accordance with its plain meaning, while also alluding to a deeper wisdom. The Torah is referred to as "golden apples plated with silver,"[428] because it is precious both on the inside and the outside. The outside of the Torah is the plain meaning of the Written Torah, which is precious like silver, while the inside of the Torah is the hidden meaning of the words of the Torah, which is precious like gold.[429] Both sides of the Torah are equally true and contain Divine wisdom.

According to the midrash, when Yisrael proclaimed, "We will do and we will hear," they accepted only the Written Torah, not the Oral Torah.[430] The *Chasam Sofer* explains that B'nei Yisrael did not reject the Oral Torah outright, but they were more circumspect in their acceptance: they wished to first acquaint themselves with its contents before committing themselves to it. Since Hashem did not wish for the Oral

---

427 *Seforno, Parashas Mishpatim* 24:12.
428 *Sefer Mishlei* 25:11.
429 Rabbeinu Bachya, *Parashas Bo* 13:1.
430 *Midrash Tanchuma, Parashas Noach.*

Torah to be accepted in a conditional manner, He forced the Oral Torah upon them. He held the mountain over their heads, saying,[431] If you accept the Torah, fine, but if not, you will be buried here."[432]

How can it be that the Jewish nation did not fully embrace the Oral Torah? The Written Torah without the Oral Torah is incomprehensible! It would be impossible to perform even one mitzvah properly without the Oral Torah, which sheds light on the details of each mitzvah. Even the mitzvah of Shabbos, which is mentioned numerous times in the Written Torah, is indecipherable without guidance from the Oral Torah, as the Mishnah states: "*Hilchos Shabbos, Chagigos,* and *Meilos* are like mountains hanging on a thread."[433] There is scant support in the text of the Written Torah for the numerous *halachos* of these mitzvos. For example, without the Oral Torah illuminating the way for us, we would have no way of distinguishing between the *melachos* that are forbidden on Shabbos and those that are permitted.

Even those mitzvos that have a strong base in the text of the Written Torah would be unintelligible without the Oral Torah. The halachic details of *tzaraas* and of the *avodah* in the Holy Temple are covered in great detail in the Torah, but without the Oral Torah that elaborates on these *halachos*, our understanding of these mitzvos would be woefully insufficient.

Furthermore, the Talmud asserts: "Hashem established a covenant with Yisrael only on the Oral Torah."[434] The definition of a covenant is a willing commitment on both sides. If Hashem made a covenant with Yisrael over the Oral Torah, it must have been accepted willingly, not by force.

Given the above, and considering its centrality to living as Jews, how could our acceptance of the Torah not have also included the Oral Torah?

The Jewish People did, in fact, wholeheartedly accept the Oral Torah taught to them by Moshe. They believed with all of their heart that the Torah Moshe conveyed to them was from Hashem. However, the Oral

---

431   *Rashi, Parashas Yisro* 19:17.
432   *Teshuvos Chasam Sofer, Orach Chaim* §208, see also *Ohr HaChaim, Parashas Yisro* 19:5.
433   *Maseches Chagigah* 10a.
434   *Maseches Gittin* 60b.

Torah includes not only the Torah taught by Moshe, but also the Torah that would be taught to them by the Torah leaders of future generations. The Jewish People were not so quick to accept the Oral Torah that would be taught to them by the sages who would come to prominence in later generations.

After the Revelation at Mount Sinai, Hashem continued transmitting Torah to Yisrael. Upon the building of the *Mishkan*, Hashem transmitted Torah from between the *keruvim* on top of the Holy Ark in the Holy of Holies. The voice of Hashem conveying Torah could be heard from the *Ohel Mo'ed*, but it only reached the ears of Moshe, while the rest of B'nei Yisrael were unable to hear it.[435] Not just Moshe, but the Torah leaders throughout the ages have been privy to the ongoing transmission of the Torah. When the Jewish People accepted the Torah with the words, "We will do and we will hear," they accepted not only the Torah they heard at Mount Sinai, but also the Torah taught to them by Moshe, after the Revelation at Sinai. But they were not as willing to accept the Torah that would be taught to them by the Torah sages who would arise after Moshe's death.

The *Chasam Sofer* explains that there was an essential difference between the transmission of the Torah through Moshe and that of the leaders of subsequent generations. The Torah was transmitted to Moshe by means of prophecy; Moshe continued to hear the direct voice of Hashem from the *Ohel Mo'ed* even after *Matan* Torah. However, after Moshe's death, the Torah could no longer be conveyed to Yisrael through prophecy. It is prohibited to introduce new Torah laws after the death of Moshe by way of prophecy because[436] "[The Torah] is not in Heaven."[437]

However, that does not mean that Hashem stopped transmitting Torah to the world; He continues to transmit Torah to the Torah leaders

---

435 *Rashi, Parashas Vayikra* 1:1.
436 *Parashas Nitzavim* 30:12. The *Chasam Sofer* maintains that the concept that new Torah laws may not be introduced by means of prophecy is the foundation of the entire Torah, because otherwise, anyone can claim that he is a prophet and that he was told from Heaven that one or more mitzvos no longer apply. This concern doesn't pertain to Moshe, however, because the entire Torah is based on Moshe's prophecy and Moshe introduced Torah laws by means of prophecy.
437 *Maseches Shabbos* 104a.

by means of *ruach hakodesh* (Divine inspiration). The Torah leaders of each generation are blessed with Divinely inspired wisdom, which allows them to introduce novel Torah laws using the thirteen rules for expounding the Torah.[438] This change was immediately apparent upon the death of Moshe. During the mourning period for Moshe, the Jewish People forgot three thousand Torah laws taught to them by Moshe.[439] Hashem did not convey these laws to Moshe's successor Yehoshua bin Nun as a prophecy, but instead, Osniel ben Kenaz managed to retrieve the forgotten laws by way of his incisive analyses.[440]

Chazal teach: "Although prophecy was taken away from the Prophets (after the destruction of the Beis Hamikdash), it was not taken away from the sages."[441] The sages were blessed with Divine inspiration, which gave them the insight to plumb the depths of the Torah and extract novel Torah laws that can be found underneath the surface. This Divine inspiration was not removed from the Torah sages even after the end of the era of prophecy,[442] as the Talmud teaches: "A sage is greater than a prophet."[443]

This is not dependent on the stature of the particular generation or particular leader. The Torah sages of every generation are greater than prophets and their words must be heeded. Chazal teach: "Yeruba'al [Gideon] in his generation is like Moshe in his generation, B'dan [Shimshon] in his generation is like Aharon in his generation, and Yiftach in his generation is like Shmuel [HaNavi] in his generation."[444] Despite the towering greatness of Moshe, Aharon, and Shmuel,[445] Yeruba'al, B'dan, and Yiftach, as leaders of Yisrael, are considered the equals of Moshe, Aharon, and Shmuel because each generation is given a leader that is suitable for that generation. The leader of each generation is attuned to the ongoing transmission of Torah, just like Moshe.

---

438   *Teshuvos Chasam Sofer, Orach Chaim* §208.

439   *Maseches Temurah* 16a.

440   Ibid.

441   *Maseches Bava Basra* 12a.

442   *Ramban*, ibid.

443   *Bava Basra* 12a.

444   *Maseches Rosh Hashanah* 25b.

445   The Talmud maintains that Shmuel was equal to Moshe and Aharon (*Maseches Berachos* 31b).

Nevertheless, Yisrael's eager commitment to the Torah did not include the Torah taught to them by the Torah leaders of future generations. Moshe heard the Torah directly from Hashem and the Jewish People were confident that the mitzvos given to them by Moshe would not be too difficult to keep. They lacked the same confidence in the mitzvos that would be given to them by the sages of future generations. They were afraid that the Rabbinic mitzvos that the sages conveyed would not be Hashem's will, and the mitzvos would prove difficult to keep.[446] Nevertheless, Hashem compelled them to accept the dictates of all future prophets by holding Mount Sinai over their heads and threatening them with death.[447]

Despite the difficulty in accepting them, we must heed the words of the sages in the same manner that we heed the words of the Torah. The Torah instructs us: "Do not stray from their words that they teach you to the right or to the left,"[448] meaning, even if it appears to us that the sages are instructing us that right is left or left is right, we must heed their words.[449] We must put aside our own mind and will and follow the dictates of the sages in the same manner that Yitzchak allowed himself to be led to the *Akeidah,* on the basis of the prophecy of his father Avraham. When we adhere to the words of the sages, we are recreating the mitzvah of the *Akeidah,* and we merit for ourselves the blessing that Hashem gave to Avraham after the *Akeidah,* "I will multiply your children like the stars in heaven and like the sand that is on the edge of the sea."[450]

With this, we gain a better understanding of the decree of the sages not to blow the shofar on Rosh Hashanah when it falls out on Shabbos.[451] Chazal tell us that the mitzvah of the shofar awakens for us the merit of the *Akeidah,* and that merit stands for us when we stand in judgment

---

446   *Teshuvos Chasam Sofer* §205.
447   *Maseches Shabbos* 88a.
448   *Parashas Shoftim* 17:11.
449   *Rashi,* ibid.
450   *Parashas Vayeira* 22:17.
451   *Maseches Rosh Hashanah* 29b.

in front of Hashem.[452] When the first day of Rosh Hashanah falls out on Shabbos, we do not have that merit on the day of justice. So what merit do we bring with us when we stand in front of Hashem to be judged? The answer is that when Rosh Hashanah falls on a weekday, we bring only the ancient merit of the *Akeidah* in front of Hashem, but when it falls on a Shabbos, we merit anew the self-sacrifice of the *Akeidah*. When we adhere to the words of the sages and abstain from blowing the shofar on Shabbos Rosh Hashanah, just as Yitzchak adhered to his father Avraham and allowed him to bring him as a sacrifice, we are recreating the mitzvah of the *Akeidah*. We don't just have the merit of the original *Akeidah*, but the merit of our own *Akeidah*!

---

452 Ibid.

THE JEWISH PEOPLE accepted whole-heartedly both the Written and Oral Torah taught to them by Moshe. They were more restrained in their acceptance of the Torah that would be taught to them by the sages of future generations, out of fear that it would prove too difficult for them to keep. Nevertheless, Hashem held the mountain over their heads and compelled them to keep it.

TWENTY-SIX

KIYEMU V'KIBLU

While Yisrael did not originally accept the Torah of the sages that would come after Moshe, this willing acceptance would ultimately occur during the Babylonian exile, after the destruction of the First Holy Temple.

The Jewish nation wholeheartedly accepted the Torah upon experiencing the miracles of the Purim story. The Talmud learns this from the words *"kiyemu v'kiblu"* in *Megillas Esther*,[453] which means that the Jewish nation affirmed what they had previously accepted[454] under duress at Mount Sinai. Prior to this, the Jewish People had accepted the Oral Torah taught to them by Moshe, but they had not agreed to accept the edicts of the Torah sages of future generations. The edicts of the sages of all generations are an integral part of the Oral Torah, and the acceptance of the Oral Torah is predicated on a full acceptance of them. Only after the Purim story did the Jewish People willingly accept these edicts.

What occurred at that time that prompted Yisrael to accept the Oral Torah taught by all future sages? To understand this, it would be helpful to review the function and purpose of the Rabbinic mitzvos.

As we mentioned earlier, the Rabbinic mitzvos were established for the purpose of keeping the Jewish People from straying from the

---

453 *Megillas Esther* 9:27.
454 *Maseches Shabbos* 88a.

path of the Torah. As such, the Rabbinic mitzvos are dependent on the standing of the Jewish People at a particular time and generation. In the immediate aftermath of the Revelation at Sinai, few Rabbinic mitzvos were needed because of the elevated spiritual standing of the Jewish People. However, with the passage of generations and the inevitable decline of the Jewish People's spiritual standing, additional Rabbinic mitzvos were added.[455]

The sages were blessed with Divine inspiration, which directed them to convey new Rabbinic mitzvos as needed for their generation. The acceptance of the Oral Torah is based on faith in the sages and their role in the transmission of the mitzvos. Faith in the sages and the Divine inspiration that guides them is predicated on two fundamental beliefs:

- A belief in Divine Providence: The belief that Hashem is cognizant of every change in our spiritual standing and that He conveys to the sages additional Rabbinic mitzvos to address this.
- A belief in Divine inspiration: The belief that as a consequence of their sanctity and fear of Hashem, the sages are blessed with Divine inspiration that guides them in their conveyance of the Rabbinic mitzvos.

The Divine Providence that the Jewish People experienced upon their salvation from Haman's plot demonstrated to them that even in the deep darkness of exile, Hashem was still with them. The Jewish nation at that time was scattered throughout the world, as Haman said, "There is one nation who is scattered among the nations." [456] The Presence of Hashem was hidden from them as a fulfillment of the prophecy of "I will hide my face from them."[457] Yet, their miraculous salvation from Haman's evil plot demonstrated that even in their sorry state, Hashem was still with them.

Not only is Hashem with the Jewish People in exile, but Divine Providence is intensified. The Talmud tells us that when Yisrael is exiled, Hashem exiles Himself with them and when they return from

---

455   Rav Mordechai Neugroschel, *Sefer V'Hasheivosa El Levavecha*.
456   *Megillas Esther* 3:8.
457   *Parashas Haazinu* 32:20.

exile, Hashem returns with them.[458] When Yisrael is in exile, Hashem does not abandon them even for a moment because that would spell their destruction. This is in contrast to the state of affairs while Yisrael was still living in Eretz Yisrael; they were governed in accordance with their respective merits, and when they sinned, Hashem abandoned them and left them to their fate.[459] The intensity of Divine Providence that the Jewish nation experiences in exile allows them to survive and even thrive, even while they are scattered among the nations and under constant threat of annihilation.

The miracle of the Purim story instilled in the Jewish People this concept that Hashem is with them at all times, even in the darkest days of exile. The reality that Hashem is with the Jewish People even when His Presence seems hidden instilled in the Jewish People the belief in the sages and the mitzvos that they enacted. They recognized that Hashem's Presence is perpetually with them and that He is cognizant of every change in their spiritual standing. Consequently, they believed that He would address any spiritual decline with the transmission of additional Rabbinic mitzvos by the Torah sages of each generation.

The events of the Purim story also brought the Jewish People to the recognition of the Divine inspiration that guides the Torah sages in everything they do. Rav Eliyahu Dessler explains:[460] Mordechai forbade the Jewish People from attending Achashveirosh's party, which he held for the entire population of his kingdom. Mordechai's edict was in the category of a Rabbinic mitzvah, which the people were obligated to keep. Nevertheless, the people refused to adhere to Mordechai's edict on the grounds that all other nations were attending, and their absence would put them in danger of retribution from the king. Nine years later, Mordechai refused to bow down to Haman, despite an explicit command from Achashveirosh to do so. The Jewish People warned Mordechai that he was putting them in danger, but he paid no heed. Soon after, Haman's anger at Mordechai's defiance drove him to request

---

458   *Maseches Megillah* 29a.
459   *Parashas Vayeilech* 31:17.
460   *Michtav Mi'Eliyahu, chelek* 1.

permission from Achashveirosh to wipe out the Jewish People, and his request was granted.

The true reason for this decree was that it was a punishment for the Jewish People's defiance of Mordechai's edict with their attendance at Achashveirosh's party. However, superficially it seemed that the reason for the decree was Mordechai's refusal to bow down to Haman, and the people could easily have blamed Mordechai for the danger they were in. Nevertheless, they humbled themselves and not only did they not blame the edict on Mordechai, they also followed Mordechai's directives to fast for three consecutive days, including the first day of Pesach (a day when fasting is normally forbidden), and repent their ways. Upon witnessing the miraculous reversal of fortune for Mordechai and Esther, and how Haman's plot turned against him and led to his downfall, they arrived at a full awareness of Mordechai's righteousness and the Divine inspiration that had guided him throughout these events. They now recognized the truth: that it was their defiance of Mordechai's edict forbidding them to attend Achashveirosh's party that had brought the potential disaster upon them, and it was their subsequent repentance and adherence to Mordechai's edict to fast for three days that brought about the reversal of the decree. This recognition opened their eyes to the special Divine inspiration that the sages merit, and gave them a newfound appreciation for the sages and the Rabbinic mitzvos they enact. They now accepted all the Rabbinic mitzvos: past, present, and future.

Yisrael's full acceptance of the Oral Torah paved the way for the flourishing of the Torah that existed during the years of the Second Holy Temple, which was rebuilt soon after. The verse in *Megillas Esther* states, "For the Jews there was light and happiness and joy and glory";[461] "light" is a reference to the Torah, as the Jewish nation had now accepted willingly all of the Oral Torah — something they had previously not accomplished. The Jewish People's willing acceptance of the Oral Torah was followed by their return to Eretz Yisrael for the rebuilding of the Second Holy Temple. They were led into Eretz Yisrael by Ezra

---

461 *Megillas Esther* 8:16.

HaSofer, about whom Chazal declared that if the Torah had not already been given through Moshe, it would have been given through him.[462] In fact, Ezra HaSofer brought about a noteworthy change to the Torah: the letters of the *Sefer Torah* were altered to *k'sav ashuris* (Assyrian script).[463] A significant feature of *k'sav ashuris* is the *"tagin"* — the crowns of the letters. The midrash relates that Rabbi Akiva expounded on every speck of the crowns of the letters and learned numerous *halachos* from them. In fact, Torah concepts that were not revealed to Moshe were revealed to Rabbi Akiva and his colleagues.[464] This additional wisdom that lay within the crowns, by which Torah laws that were hidden even from Moshe could be derived, was brought to light as a result of B'nei Yisrael's willing acceptance of the Oral Torah, something that had not occurred in Moshe's time.

The generation that returned from the Babylonian exile and rebuilt the Holy Temple was the last generation of prophecy. The prophets Chagai, Zechariah, and Malachi were the last of the Prophets, and upon their deaths, the era of prophecy drew to a close. However, this did not in any way impede the ongoing transmission of the Oral Torah, as the Oral Torah is not transmitted via prophecy, but rather by means of Divine inspiration and the wisdom of the sages. Although many of the earlier sages were prophets, they did not transmit the Torah through prophecy, but rather through Divine inspiration. In contrast to prophecy, Divine inspiration never ceased, and thus the transmission of the Torah continued unabated into the post-prophecy era. The post-prophecy era ushered in a new, even greater era for the transmission of the Oral Torah, as Chazal teach: "A sage is greater than a prophet."[465]

This proliferation of the Oral Torah culminated in the compilation of the six orders of the Mishnah and the *Beraisa*, which is the essence of the Oral Torah, by Rabbi Yehudah HaNasi and his students. This was followed by the era of the Talmud, which consists of the *Talmud*

462　*Maseches Sanhedrin* 21b.
463　Ibid.
464　*Bamidbar Rabbah, perek* 19.
465　*Maseches Bava Basra* 12b.

Yerushalmi and *Bavli* and is the elaboration of the Mishnah. The *Bavli*, or Babylonian Talmud — the more authoritative of the two — was compiled by Ravina and Rav Ashi along with their students.

However, says Rav Avigdor Miller, despite the greatness of the era, Yisrael did not reach their potential. The refusal of the majority of Yisrael to join Ezra HaSofer when he ascended to Eretz Yisrael spoiled the great opportunity this presented, as Chazal relates, "Yisrael deserved a miracle at the time of Ezra just as they did at the time of Yehoshua bin Nun, if not for the sin."[466] They sinned in their refusal to ascend to Eretz Yisrael, and the potential that existed was thus wasted. Nevertheless, the insistence of the majority to remain in Babylon was to some extent a part of Hashem's plan for the proliferation of the Oral Torah. The Talmud relates, "Hashem foresaw that Yisrael could not withstand the cruel oppression of Rome, and he therefore exiled them (kept them in exile) to Bavel."[467] The Babylonian and Persian rulers displayed exceptional benevolence to the Jewish community living in their kingdoms. The large and vigorous population of Babylonian Jewry was therefore able to continue as a Torah reservoir that constantly replenished the community in Judah. Therefore, Yeshayah HaNavi declared, "In the days to come, Yaakov shall take root, Yisrael shall blossom and produce flowers, and the world shall become full of its fruit."[468] It was the delightful fragrance and the luscious fruit of the Babylonian Talmud that was destined to fill the world. [469]

---

466   *Maseches Berachos* 4a.
467   *Maseches Pesachim* 87b.
468   *Sefer Yeshayah* 27:6.
469   Rav Avigdor Miller in *Torah Nation*.

THE JEWISH PEOPLE recognized the Divine Providence in the exile of Babylon in a way that they never recognized in Eretz Yisrael. This brought them to a newfound appreciation of the Torah sages and their role in the transmission of the Rabbinic mitzvos, and they now accepted upon themselves all of the mitzvos instituted by the Torah sages past, present, and future.

AFTERWORD

The Jewish nation finally accepted the Oral Torah at the time of the Purim story. Upon their subsequent return to Eretz Yisrael and the rebuilding of the Holy Temple, the Oral Torah flourished. Nevertheless, the Second Holy Temple did not have the same level of sanctity as the First Holy Temple, as five holy items were missing: the Holy Ark, the fire that descended from Heaven, the Presence of Hashem, *ruach hakodesh*, and the *urim v'tumim*.[470] But what the Jewish People lost in holiness, they gained in unity. The Jewish People were unified in a way that hadn't existed during the time of the First Holy Temple, as a result of their common loyalty to the Torah sages.

Unfortunately, that unity began to unravel toward the end of the Second Holy Temple. Chazal tell us that the Second Holy Temple was destroyed as a result of senseless hate. At first glance, this doesn't seem to be a particularly egregious sin that would warrant the destruction of the Holy Temple. This is especially true when considering the sins that caused the destruction of the First Temple — the three cardinal sins of idolatry, forbidden relations, and murder. However, upon deeper introspection into the nature of the First and Second Holy Temples, we can understand why these sins in particular caused their destruction.

The *Maharal* explains[471] that the First Holy Temple was given to us in the merit of our great forefathers, Avraham, Yitzchak, and Yaakov. This

---

470   *Maseches Yoma* 21b.
471   *Sefer Netzach Yisrael* chap 4.

provided great sanctity to the First Holy Temple and made it a resting place for the Divine Presence. However, the prevalence of the three cardinal sins of idolatry, forbidden relations, and murder profaned its sanctity and it was no longer suited to be a resting place for the Divine Presence. With the expulsion of the Divine Presence, the Holy Temple was vulnerable to destruction by the Babylonians.

The Second Holy Temple was not sanctified in the same way as the First Temple. The Talmud tells us that the Jewish People no longer had the merit of the forefathers after the destruction of the First Holy Temple and without that merit, the original sanctity could not be completely restored. Instead, says the *Maharal*, the Second Holy Temple existed in the merit of the Jewish People as a unified nation. The merit of their newfound acceptance of Torah sages and the Rabbinic mitzvos they enacted was a great spiritual force that brought in the Divine Presence. The Mishnah tells us that when ten people gather together to engage in Torah learning, they are graced with the Divine Presence.[472] The Jewish People united around the Torah sages for the purpose of learning Torah, and this brought a level of sanctity to the Holy Temple. Since the Second Holy Temple existed in the merit of our unity as a nation, when we engaged in senseless hate it undermined our unity and stripped the Holy Temple of its sanctity. This resulted in the destruction of the Holy Temple by the Romans.

How do we regain the unity that we lost upon the destruction of the Holy Temple? When we unite around the Torah sages and humble ourselves in front of them, this helps us achieve unity with our fellow man and with Hashem. Thus, in the aftermath of the destruction of the Beis Hamikdash, Rabbi Yochanan ben Zakai requested from the Roman Caesar: "Give me Yavneh and its sages."[473] Rabbi Yochanan knew that only with the survival of the sages could the healing process of the destruction begin. We no longer have the sages of Yavneh, but the Torah scholars of our generation are no less precious, because Hashem gives

---

472   *Pirkei Avos* 3:6.
473   *Maseches Gittin* 56b.

each generation the Torah scholars that are most suitable for that generation. By humbling ourselves to the Torah sages and adhering to their words, we have the ability to achieve the unity that will bring Mashiach, may it be soon in our days.

GLOSSARY

Adam	The first man.
adam	A person.
Adon	Lord; a name sometimes used in reference to Hashem.
Aggadah	Passages written by the Sages relating events, expounding verses, or teaching ethics.
Akeidah	Binding, usually a reference to Avraham's binding of Yitzchak for the purpose of bringing him as a sacrifice.
am bazui	An inferior nation.
arel	Uncircumcised.
av hamon goyim	Father of a multitude of nations.
Avinu	Our father.
avodah zarah	Idolatry.
avodah	Service of Hashem; the bringing of sacrifices in the Holy Temple; prayer.
Avos	Fathers, forefathers; tractate of the Mishnah.
B'nei	Children of.
Beis Hamikdash	The Holy Temple.
batei midrashos	Study halls of Torah.
bayis ne'eman b'Yisrael	A house of faith in Yisrael.

bechor	Firstborn son.
beis din	Jewish court.
beis hasefer	School for learning Torah.
ben	Son of.
ben Noach/B'nei Noach	Lit., the son(s) of Noach; a non-Yisrael.
Beraisa	Mishnaic-era explanatory teachings.
Birkas Hamazon	After-blessing on bread.
bitachon	Security in the belief that Hashem is with us and does only good for us.
B'nei Noach	Children of Noach.
B'nei Yisrael	Lit., the sons of Yisrael; the Jewish nation.
bris milah	Circumcision.
Chagigos	*Chagigah* sacrifice brought on the Jewish holidays of Pesach, Shavuos, and Sukkos.
chassidei umos ha'olam	Righteous among the nations.
Chazal	Torah sages.
chessed	Kindness; charitable giving.
chok/chukos	Mitzvos without an obvious reason.
derech eretz	Code of proper conduct.
Dinim	Statutes.
Eidos	Mitzvos that are a testimonial for an event.
eikev	Heel.
Eitz HaChaim	Lit., tree of life; tree in Gan Eden.
Eitz HaDaas	Lit., tree of knowledge; tree in Gan Eden.
eitz	Stick; tree.
emunah	Faith.
eretz	Land.
Eretz Canaan	Land of Canaan.
Eretz Yisrael	Land of Israel.

galgal noteh m'kav mashve hayom
A circle deviating from the equator line.

Gan Eden	Garden of Eden.
gid hanasheh	Sciatic nerve.

ha'adam hagadol b'anakim
A person who is great among giants.

Haflagah	Lit., a split; a reference to the generation in which the people were split up into distinct nations.
Haggadah shel Pesach	Book recounting the Exodus from Egypt, read at the Seder on Passover.
Ha'Ivri	From the other side.
halachah/halachos	Torah law(s).
Hallel	Song of praise to Hashem from *Sefer Tehillim*.
HaMelech	The king.
HaNavi	The prophet.
HaRishon	The first.
HaSofer	The scribe.
histapkus b'muat	Eschewing excessive materialism.
ibur hashanah	A leap year.
kav	A measure.
Kel Shakai	One of the names of Hashem.
keruvim	Cherubs situated on the top of the Holy Ark in the Holy of Holies.
kibud av v'eim	Honoring one's father and mother.
kiddush ha'chodesh	Sanctifying the new moon and determining the day of Rosh Chodesh.
Kiddush	The blessing recited over a cup of wine to sanctify the Sabbath and Festivals.
kiyemu v'kiblu	Affirmed and accepted.

Kohen/Kohanim	Member(s) of the priestly caste.
korban	A sacrifice.
korban olah	A sacrifice burned entirely on the Altar in the Holy Temple.
korban Pesach	Passover sacrifice.
k'sav ashuris	Assyrian script.
k'sav ivri	Hebrew script.
l'fum tzara agra	The reward that one receives (for the mitzvos that one does) is commensurate with the degree of difficulty in keeping them.
ma'adim	*Mazal* of destruction.
ma'aminim	Believers.
ma'aseh avos siman l'banim	
	The occurrences of the forefathers foretell the future occurrences of the descendants.
mabul	Great Flood; deluge.
malach	Angel in Heaven.
Mashiach	The Messiah.
Matan Torah	The giving of the Torah on Mount Sinai.
mazal/mazalos	Constellation(s).
Megillas Esther	Scroll of Esther.
Meilos	The profaning of objects of sanctity.
melachos	Types of labor forbidden by the Torah on the Sabbath and Festivals.
midrash	Non-literal interpretations or homiletic teachings of the sages; an exposition (or compilation of expositions) of a scriptural verse.
Mikra	Verse(s) in the Torah.
Milchemes	The war of.
Mishkan	The Tabernacle.

Mishnah	The codified Oral Law, redacted by Rabbi Yehudah HaNasi; specific paragraphs of the Oral Law.
mishpatim	Mitzvos with an apparent reason.
mitzvah	Torah commandment.
Mizbei'ach	Altar; the place where the sacrifices are brought in the Holy Temple.
mo'adim	Jewish holidays.
mulim	Circumcised.
nayach	Humble.
neta revai	The mitzvah to bring the fruits of a tree's fourth year to Yerushalayim.
nevius	Prophecy.
Ohel Mo'ed	Meeting tent.
olah temimah	An unblemished *olah* sacrifice.
orlah	The prohibition of eating the fruit of a newly planted tree for the first three years.
parah adumah	Red heifer.
parashah	Section of the Torah.
peirush	Commentary.
Pesach	Festival of Passover.
Rabbeinu	Our Rabbi.
Rav	Rabbi.
Rosh Chodesh	Lit., head (first day) of the month.
ruach hakodesh	Divine inspiration.
safek	Doubt.
Sanhedrin	Supreme Jewish court.
Sar	Nobleman.
sefer	Book.
Sefer Torah	Torah scroll.

Shabbos	The Sabbath; the seventh day of the week.
sheva mitzvos b'nei Noach	
	Seven Noachide Laws.
Shevatim	The (twelve) tribes of Yisrael.
shevet	One of the tribes of Yisrael.
Sukkos	Festival of Tabernacles.
tagin	Crowns on top of the letters in a *Sefer Torah*.
Talmud Bavli	Babylonian Talmud.
Talmud	The basic corpus of Jewish law (200 BCE–500 CE), consisting of the Mishnah and Gemara.
Talmud Yerushalmi	Jerusalem Talmud.
tamim	Whole; humble.
timtum halev	Tainting of the heart.
Targum	Any one of several Aramaic translations of the Torah.
teva	Nature.
tohu v'vohu	Void and emptiness.
Torah	Lit., law or teaching; the corpus of Sinaitic tradition, encompassing the Written and Oral Laws; also used to refer to the Five Books of Moses.
tzaraas	Leprosy.
tzeduki	A heretic who believes only in the Written Torah, not the Oral Torah.
tzur	A rock.
urim v'tumim	Lit., light and complete; a parchment inscribed with the explicit name of Hashem that was inserted between the folds of the *choshen* (breastplate) and worn by the *Kohen Gadol*.
yashar/yashrus	One who acts with exemplary behavior.
yeridas hadoros	The spiritual decline from one generation to the next.

Yerushalayim	Jerusalem.
Yisrael mumar	A wayward Jew.
Yisrael	A Jewish person; the Jewish nation.

About the Author

Rabbi Chaim Brown was born and raised in Baltimore, Maryland, and learned in Yeshivas Ner Yisroel and Mir Yerushalayim. He has served as a *magid shiur* on the Shema Yisrael Torah Network and as a contributor to the Daf Yomi Advancement Forum. He resides with his family in Ramat Beit Shemesh, Israel.

ABOUT MOSAICA PRESS

Mosaica Press is an independent publisher of Jewish books. Our authors include some of the most profound, interesting, and entertaining thinkers and writers in the Jewish community today. Our books are available around the world. Please visit us at www.mosaicapress.com or contact us at info@mosaicapress.com. We will be glad to hear from you.